Logical Database
Design Principles

Logical Database Design Principles

John Garmany
Jeff Walker
Terry Clark

Auerbach Publications
Taylor & Francis Group
Boca Raton   London   New York   Singapore

Published in 2005 by
Auerbach Publications
Taylor & Francis Group
5000 Broken Sound Parkway NW, Suite 300
Boca Raton, FL 33487-2742

© 2005 by Taylor & Francis Group, LLC
Auerbach is an imprint of Taylor & Francis Group

No claim to original U.S. Government works
Printed in the United States of America on acid-free paper
10 9 8 7 6 5 4 3 2 1

International Standard Book Number-10: 0-8493-1853-X (Hardcover)
International Standard Book Number-13: 978-0-8493-1853-5 (Hardcover)
Library of Congress Card Number 2004061916

Library of Congress Cataloging-in-Publication Data

Garmany, John
   Logical database design principles / John Garmany, Jeff Walker, Terry Clark.
      p. cm. -- (Foundations of database design series)
   Includes index.
   ISBN 0-8493-1853-X (alk. paper)
   1. Database design. I. Walker, Jeff. II. Clark, Terry. III. Title. IV. Series.

QA76.9.D26G37 2005
005.74--dc22   2004061916

Taylor & Francis Group
is the Academic Division of T&F Informa plc.

Visit the Taylor & Francis Web site at
http://www.taylorandfrancis.com

and the Auerbach Publications Web site at
http://www.auerbach-publications.com

DEDICATION

This book is dedicated to Don Burleson
for all his support and assistance.

John Garmany and Terry Clark

I dedicate this book to my wife, whose loving support and
encouragement made it all possible.

Jeff Walker

CONTENTS

ACKNOWLEDGMENTS

I want to acknowledge the help and expertise received from my fellow faculty members at the University of South Florida, the University of Tampa, and St. Petersburg College.

Jeff Walker

Creating a book is a group task that requires the support of many people. This book has undergone a number of changes both in content and in format since Auerbach agreed to publish it. Writing a book while working full time can be a daunting task and coordinating three authors just adds to the excitement. A special thanks to Rich O'Hanley and Auerbach Publishing for sticking with us through constant delays.

And a special thanks to the editing and publishing staff led by John Wyzalek and Gerry Jaffe who took this manuscript and created the book. Great job!

Lastly, we must thank our co-workers, who provided both guidance and support, not to mention picking up the slack as we dedicated time to writing the book.

John Garmany, Jeff Walker, and Terry Clark

INTRODUCTION

We have worked for many years as consultants in the information industry, mostly focusing on helping companies maintain their data and database management systems (DBMSs). Most companies focus on their application, leaving the database design to a DBA (database administrator), who ends up just trying to get the DBMS to function fast enough to stop complaints. In fact, many vendors have implemented features to allow the database to change the way a DBMS executes queries, even to the point where a DBA can substitute an efficient query for a poorly written application query from inside the database.

However, for a DBMS to efficiently support the storage and retrieval of company data, the schema design must be implemented with an understanding of the structure of the data and how it will be accessed. The logical design allows one to analyze the data itself. Once one has the logical design, one needs to move to the physical design. The physical design is based on the capabilities of the DBMS selected to host the data.

Logical database design principles have been around for many years and there are a number of books on the topic. The inspiration for this book came about because almost all design books focused exclusively on relational design. However, modern database management systems have added powerful features that have caused a movement away from truly normalized database design. This book is basically a reflection of what we have encountered in recent years working in the information industry.

What we tried to do is start with the traditional logical design principles, normalizing and modeling the data, then progress into designing for specific purposes such as object-oriented, online transaction processing (OLTP), and data warehouses. The reader will notice that as we moved away from relational design, we were forced to move away from the purely logical into some of the physical design. This was required because of the way many of the features of modern databases are implemented. In the case of object-oriented databases, one will find that the application design, in fact, drives the database schema design. Hopefully, they will be designed together but that is frequently not the case. Some database features can be implemented during the transition from logical design to physical design. However, many (such as data warehousing) will benefit by analyzing demoralization in the logical design.

Finally, because this is a logical design book, we tried to make the examples database-neutral. Because each vendor has implemented features in different ways, we were sometimes forced to use examples from a specific DBMS. When required, we selected an example that most clearly demonstrated the concept being discussed.

ABOUT THE AUTHORS

John Garmany

John Garmany is a graduate of West Point and a retired LTC with 20+ years of IT experience. John is an OCP Certified Oracle DBA with a Master's degree in information systems, a Graduate Certificate in software engineering, and a B.S. degree (electrical engineering) from West Point. He is Senior Consultant with Burleson Enterprise, Inc., and author of the *Oracle Replication Handbook* by Rampant TechPress and *Oracle10g Application Server Handbook* by Oracle Press.

Terry Clark

Terry Clark is an Oracle Certified DBA with more than 25 years of full-time IT experience. Certified in client/server and LAN technologies by DePaul University, Terry has extensive experience troubleshooting and tuning database networks. An acknowledged Oracle Windows expert, Terry has published in *Oracle Internals Magazine* and has over a decade of Oracle experience working with mission-critical Oracle systems.

Jeff Walker

As an instructor at St. Petersburg College, Jeff led the Oracle program and taught Oracle-authorized course materials to students seeking Oracle certification. He is recognized by Oracle as an Oracle Certified Application Developer and an Oracle Certified Professional Internet Application Developer. His education includes a Master's degree in business administration/contracts and Bachelor degrees in MIS and political science. He has won awards for his leadership, technical knowledge, and teaching success, including an appointment by the Governor of Florida to the Small Disadvantaged Manufacturing Corporation.

1

INTRODUCTION TO LOGICAL DATABASE DESIGN

The goal in this chapter is to define logical databases, identify the elements and structures of logical design, and describe the steps used to create that design. It sounds simple enough, but it is a lofty goal that requires more than memorizing a definition and learning the elements of logical database design. Success depends on the application of critical thinking as well as analytical and interpersonal skills.

UNDERSTANDING A DATABASE

Before starting the process of designing a logical database, we need to understand what a database is and what some of the design approaches are that distinguish one database type from another. The simplest definition of a database is a collection of data items stored for later retrieval. Notice that there is no mention of computers or database management systems. That is because databases have been around much longer than both computers and database management systems. When the first caveman etched charcoal on the cave to track the passage of time, the first database was born. In this example, the data was stored as marks on the wall and the data retrieved by looking at the wall. As technology evolved, the marks moved from the wall to a notebook, then to a filing cabinet, and later to data files in a directory on a computer. Once computers made the scene, we discovered different approaches to optimize and manage the database.

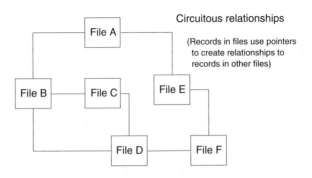

Figure 1.1 Network database model.

DATABASE ARCHITECTURES

Prior to 1969, common database architectures were based on hierarchical and network systems. We review these approaches to establish a point of comparison to better understand relational databases. The discussion is a brief one because, for all intents and purposes, these approaches are considered obsolete. This does not mean you will not find them in use, because legacy systems used by companies with high transaction rates and where data resides on mainframes still exist. Just understand that most new database systems are designed for a relational or object-relational database.

A network database system as depicted in Figure 1.1 organizes files in a manner that associates each file with n number of other files. This approach uses pointers to create a relationship between records in one file and records in another file. The network approach provides more flexibility than the hierarchical approach and allows a database designer to optimize the database using detailed control and data organization. Record types can be organized using hashing algorithms or are located near another related record type (an early form of clustering). Do not worry about these advanced terms now; they are discussed in subsequent chapters. The drawback to the network approach involves performance and overhead. Overhead is the storage and code maintenance of the database that is required to implement the relationships. Additional drawbacks include the need for significant programming skills, database design knowledge, time, plus topic-specific expertise.

Notice in Figure 1.1 that the network database model creates circuitous relationships. Each box in the diagram represents a file. The redundancy is obvious, in that each file is related to multiple files. This occurs because records in one file use pointers to records in another file.

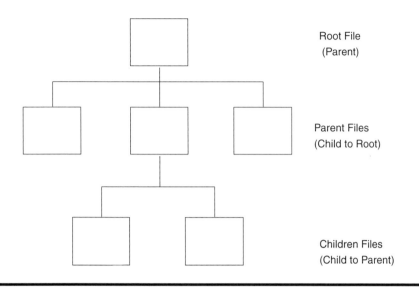

Figure 1.2   **Hierarchical database model.**

A hierarchical database system as depicted in Figure 1.2 organizes files in a top-down, branching tree architecture similar to a company's organization model. This approach associates files in a parent/child relationship. By its nature, this architecture is limited to associations derived from the top or root file and flowed down the branches. This approach has limited flexibility, as each relationship depends on the file above it. A parent record can have multiple child records, but each child record can have only one parent. The relationships are based on address pointers.

So what are some of the characteristics of both the hierarchical and network database approaches?:

- They use pointers.
- Their architecture uses redundancy to create relationships and optimization.
- They evolved over time, almost on a trial and error basis.
- Models were developed after the fact to explain and improve them, but not as part of the original design and theory.

The fact that hierarchical and network models were developed after those databases were implemented is significant. It underscores the contributions made by Dr. Edgar F. Codd, considered by most as the "father of the relational database." When he published his "Derivability, Redundancy and Consistency of Relations Stored in Large Data Banks" as an IBM Research Report in 1969, he introduced science into database management. He was the first to offer a theoretical explanation or model of data.

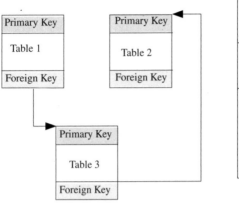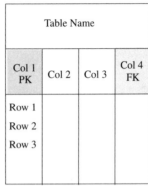

Figure 1.3   Relational database.

RELATIONAL DATABASES

OK, so what is a relational database? As depicted in Figure 1.3, it is a data model in which the data is stored in tables (also referred to as entities). Each table has rows (also referred to as records or tuples) and columns (also referred to as attributes). Each row in a table has a unique identifier (UID), which is referred to as a primary key (PK). Cross-reference links between tables can be defined by creating a FOREIGN KEY (FK) in one table that references a primary key in another table. When defined in this manner, the link or relationship provides referential integrity. That is, data must exist in the referenced table before it can be placed in the referencing table. This aspect is further discussed in subsequent chapters.

What really distinguishes a relational database from the network and hierarchical databases is that relationships are defined using the UID of one table and joining them with the UID of another table. Pointers are not used. Data redundancy is reduced via a process called normalization.

Finally, data can be accessed using Structured Query Language (SQL). Using a relational database, we can update our database definition. A database is a shared collection of logically related data items needed by an enterprise and stored on a server or distributed over several computers where data can be retrieved based on user needs.

CREATING THE DATABASE

Now knowing the database types, we could seclude ourselves in an office and create a relational database using SQL to build the tables and relationships between them. Unfortunately, this approach will result in poor performance, inefficiencies, and a database that does not meet the needs of the organization. What is needed is a methodology to discover the organization's requirements, define a specification, design a database, implement that database design, and, finally, maintain that database. Fortunately, there is a methodology; it is known as the System Development Life Cycle (SDLC).

SYSTEM DEVELOPMENT LIFE CYCLE (SDLC)

Designing a database requires an understanding of the Systems Development Life Cycle (SDLC), which is comprised of several phases: systems planning, systems analysis, systems design, systems implementation, and systems operations and support. The *planning phase* would be conducted by a systems analyst. It would include an investigation of the existing systems in the enterprise to determine how well the operations are performing as well as a feasibility study to assess the economic impact of the project and time constraints. If the planning phase returns a positive recommendation, the *systems analysis* phase would begin. In this phase, a systems analyst would identify business processes that must be done in the new system. Findings would be documented and logical models developed for the enterprise, data, processes, and objects. The end product would be a complete requirements document for the new system, along with costs, schedules, and benefits. The *systems design* phase would then translate the requirements into a specification that identified all required inputs, outputs, processes, and controls. The *systems implementation* phase would be next, and the specification identified in the design phase would be built. Developers write the programs and scripts and document the system. Trainers train users and DBAs (database administrators) implement the system in a production schema. Finally, in the *systems operation and support* phase, the IT department would maintain the system and provide fixes and enhancements as they are identified.

SYSTEMS PLANNING: ASSESSMENT AND FEASIBILITY

The phases of the SDLC can be better understood by focusing on the elements that are directly involved in the development of a logical database.

For our purposes, assume that the *systems planning* phase has ended and the systems analyst has recommended that we proceed with the project to design a new database system. Further assume that a feasibility study has been completed and management has approved the creation of a new database. Inherent in management's approval is a schedule, identification of available resources, and description of the work scope.

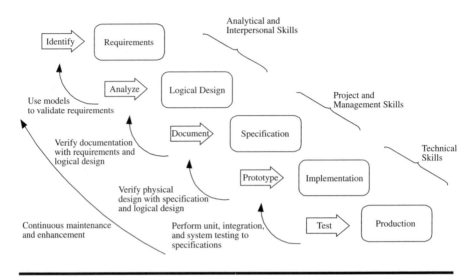

Figure 1.4 System development life cycle (SDLC).

The approval is important because it defines what work is to be done, when that work is to be completed, and what resources will be used. The work scope will become the basis for "selling off" the database. That means documenting and demonstrating that the finished product does what is described in the scope of work. Without such a document, work could continue forever as enhancements and changes are folded into the project without assessing the impact and receiving management's approval.

The SDLC phase that truly begins the logical database design is *system analysis:* the collection and analysis of data and processes an organization uses to conduct its business. This phase uses critical thinking, analytical, and interpersonal skills to identify the data and processes into a meaningful requirements document.

Figure 1.4 graphically illustrates the elements of the SDLC (with corresponding skill sets) needed to create a logical database. The methodology steps through the process, emphasizing data collection and the resulting requirements checklist, analysis and modeling of the logical design, documentation of the requirements into a specification, prototyping a database, and production with its maintenance and enhancements. An important element of the SDLC is feedback and ongoing validation or testing. Take a look at the SDLC as it applies to logical database design.

SYSTEM ANALYSIS: REQUIREMENTS

The *analysis and collection* phase begins with identifying the requirements. This task uses communication techniques and interpersonal skills that will uncover an enterprise's processes and data needs. What makes this task so difficult is that requirements must be ferreted out. A designer cannot just automate whatever policy and procedures have been documented. Formal policies and procedures tend to obscure an organization's actual or informal processes. Furthermore, there is a tendency for an organization to continue working a particular way because that is the way that particular organization has been doing it for many years. Using investigative techniques, interviews, and questionnaires, a designer or analyst will identify management, user, and process requirements. The investigation may follow the SDLC or utilize newer techniques such as Joint Application Design (JAD).

JAD is similar to an SDLC group interview for data collection. It differs because the SDLC group interview is primarily a homogeneous group (e.g., the accounting department). JAD requires all key personnel representing all disciplines, including system types, and they meet at an off-site location. Their goal is to shorten the process by gathering more data quickly and utilizing CASE tools to structure their effort. Another, more radical approach is referred to as *business process reengineering* (BPR). This approach recognizes that some organizations may require more than tweaking or enhancement of existing processes. BPR identifies key business processes (those processes that result in a measurable output) and radically changes them to optimize output. For our purposes, we will follow the SDLC model and leave JAD and BPR to another text. We want to identify existing processes and data needs and then add desired processes and data needs. A good starting point is an analysis of existing forms.

Forms document the actions and data that an organization uses to conduct its business. Determine which forms accurately depict needed data and processes. Then identify needed tasks and efforts not documented by forms; and finally, identify actions that are historical but no longer required. Next, use questionnaires and interviews to discover desired processes and data needs from management, system, and user groups. As the requirements are identified, they should be translated into graphic models. These models will aid in the design phase and provide a visible image of the logical database design. Models help the designer create the structure of the database and communicate with management and users, regarding status and requirements in processes and data.

Analytical skills will help the designer update the processes and data that an organization needs to include in the logical database. Critical thinking skills will be used to integrate an organization's requirements, thus eliminating those no longer needed, removing duplication and redundancy, adding new or more efficient processes, and streamlining data collection and retrieval.

SYSTEM ANALYSIS: REQUIREMENTS CHECKLIST

We have discussed processes and data needs of the organization as if they were independent pieces of a very large puzzle. When determining the system requirements, a checklist is a necessary element. The checklist should identify essential features that the system must satisfy to meet the needs of the enterprise. A system requirements checklist should include *inputs, outputs, processes, performance,* and *controls. Inputs* are those steps that must occur to start a process or function. A personnel requisition would be an input that starts the hiring process. *Outputs* are often expressed as reports, task lists, or other completed functions or processes such as approval or validation. Be careful to recognize that an output of one process might be the input of another process. *Processes* should identify the actions required. For example, the Human Resources (HR) department must complete a background check on new-hire applicants. *Performance* should identify measurable aspects of the system. For example, the system must accept images (pictures) for each applicant. *Controls* would address checks and constraints you want in the system. For example, only the HR department and the Supervisor of the Affected Department should have access to new-hire applications. The checklist should include all specifics or requirements for the system. In this way, you can use the checklist to determine when a database design is completed and that it meets agreed-upon criteria.

MODELS TRACKING AND SCHEDULES

Before looking at the modeling techniques used during the *analysis* and *design* phases, the designer should become familiar with the graphical tools used to track the development of the logical database. Although a project manager will do tracking and scheduling of the time and resources, the designer will have substantial input. In smaller companies, the designer may actually be the project manager. In either circumstance, a brief introduction to two of the most common tracking models follows.

Henry L. Gantt developed a bar chart display (Figure 1.5) that is used to track project status. It has been enhanced many times and may control simple to complex projects. Gantt charts display a visual status for any project. Each horizontal bar represents a task. As the task is completed, the bar is shaded. The database designer will be required to make inputs to the project manager regarding the completion status of each task. When a task falls behind, it is easy to see its impact on other tasks and corrective action, such as adding more designers, can be taken. In addition to tracking schedule, the Gantt chart can be used to track cost and accomplishments.

For example, the budget for Task 1.1 might be $2000 and the designer reports he is only 25 percent complete at the halfway point on the

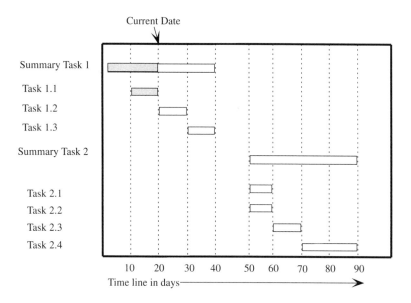

Figure 1.5   Gantt chart.

schedule. The project manager, using that data, can predict a cost overrun and a schedule delay.

Another tool for project management is the PERT or Program Evaluation Review Technique chart shown in Figure 1.6. It is similar to the Gantt but is more often used to track tasks and their inter-relationships rather than schedule. PERT is best for showing dependencies and critical paths.

PERT charts typically involve numerous contractors, departments, and organizations where the duration times are difficult to define and the relationships between the tasks are complex. Each chart starts with a task upon which all other tasks depend. Subsequent tasks are connected until a final task is completed. Each task contains a title; information about resources assigned; and best, worst, and average duration times assigned.

DESIGN MODELING

Modeling is an integral part of logical database design and, as previously discussed, is used throughout the analysis phase and will continue in the design phase. Models are graphical representations of the analysis and design, and they are communication tools that aid the designer when discussing the logical database design with users, managers, or systems personnel. More importantly, they help the designer visualize the design and validate that all processes and data needs are addressed. The different modeling techniques are discussed in detail below.

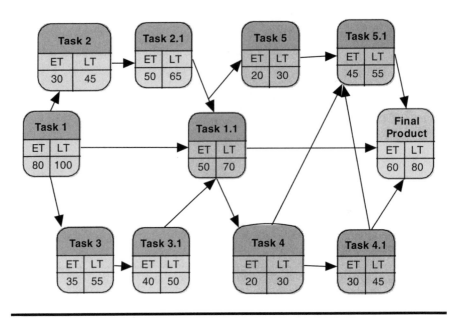

Figure 1.6 PERT chart.

FUNCTIONAL DECOMPOSITION DIAGRAM

A *functional decomposition diagram* (FDD; Figure 1.7) is like a hierarchical chart; but instead of showing the enterprise's organization, it shows the processes and functions. The FDD is a structure chart for a particular aspect of the enterprise. That is, there will be many FDDs — one for each major function or process within the organization.

The FDD in Figure 1.7 represents information collected during the *analysis* phase. The designer/analyst has determined that hiring involves the department with the open position (i.e., the Affected department), the HR department, and the Finance department. The database will have to account for these functional relationships and allow for process flow between the organizations. If the designer combines a requirements checklist with an FDD, he will know what inputs, outputs, performance, processes, and controls are needed.

In summary, the FDD can show a business function and then a breakout of lower-level functions and processes. The hiring function can be broken down to show the involvement of the HR and Finance departments as well as the Affected department in the hiring process. At a level below the Affected department, skills, personality, and budget are part of the evaluation process. Finally, the new hire must be assigned tasks and his or her performance monitored. As you design your database system, it *must* accommodate these processes and functions.

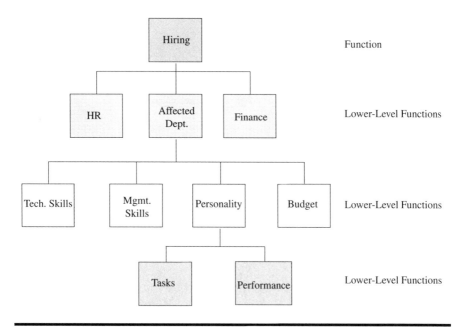

Figure 1.7   Functional decomposition diagram (FDD).

DATA FLOW DIAGRAMS

Data flow diagrams (DFDs) are used for modeling the flow of data within an organization. The "flow" is the process that data must undergo as it moves from one entity to another. As data is processed, it can be stored for future outputs. The integration of processes and data in a DFD is represented by four basic symbols: (1) processes, (2) data flows, (3) data stores, and (4) entities. The DFD in Figure 1.8 uses Yourdon and Coad symbols. There are other models that use different symbols but the DFD represents the same data, processes, storage, and entity information. Excluded from a DFD are logic steps and detail processing steps. Like the models already presented, the purpose is to provide an overview for presentations or understanding by developers of the concepts and require-ments. In a DFD, a process receives input and produces an output. For example, an applicant's qualifications constitute the input and the output produced would be a list of eligible candidates. A data flow diagram shows the path data moves from one part of the database system to another. After eligible candidates are identified, a candidate is hired. A data store represents data that the system stores for use by a process somewhere later in the database system. For example, resumés of qualified applicants are stored so that other departments can request candidate lists for positions within their departments.

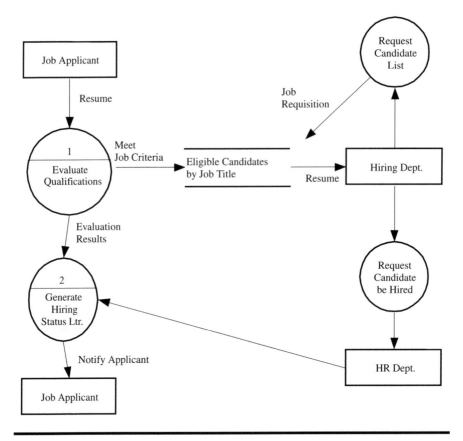

Figure 1.8   Data flow diagram (DFD).

DATA DICTIONARY

If the DFD is an overview, how is the detail modeled? The answer is that a data dictionary is created for each element of the DFD. Generally speaking, all data dictionaries include the following information:

1. *Data element name:* the name of the element as it is identified on the DFD and any other name that might be associated with the element.
2. *Data type:* identifies whether the element is a character, date, or number and the length or size of the element (e.g., 25 characters for a first name).
3. *Initial or default values:* for each data element.
4. *Validity rules:* what values are acceptable; identifies the values that should or must be used and any constraints on acceptable values; if known, states whether the valid data can be stored in a table.

Figure 1.9   Data dictionary for data flow.

5. *Source:* identifies from where a data element's values originate (does it come from a process, data store, or entity?).
6. *Security:* what limits will be placed on access; identifies which departments can access which data, and who can change, insert, or modify data.
7. *Comments:* designer notes that help conceptualize and explain the logic used to define the DFD and data dictionary.

In Figure 1.9 one can see that the data flow is detailed by creating a data store description, a data structure (record), and data elements. Documentation can be performed manually or using a CASE tool such as Visible Analyst.

Data dictionary information differs from one system to another and one analyst to another. Basic data for the data flow should include the following:

1. *Title.* What is the name of the data flow as it appears on the DFD? The first data flow in Figure 1.7 is Resumé. Is it known by any other name?
2. *Description.* What is the data flow and its purpose? In Figure 1.7, an applicant submits a resumé to the company for consideration as a new hire.
3. *Source.* Where does data flow originate? Does it come from a process, a data store, or an entity? Identify which one(s). Resumés come from outside entities known as applicants or job candidates.
4. *Destination of data flow.* Where does it go, and why? Resumés are processed by HR to evaluate the applicant's qualifications.
5. *Record.* Identify the group of data elements or data structure represented by the data flow. Data elements are often stored separately from the data flow, allowing more than one data flow to use the record (group of data elements).
6. *Volume and frequency.* Identify the number of transactions and their frequency. In our DFD, the data might involve 100 transactions per month to evaluate job seeker resumés but only 10 transactions per month for an affected department to request a list of valid candidates.

Figure 1.10 Data dictionary for external entity.

Figure 1.11 Data dictionary for processes.

In Figures 1.9, 1.10, and 1.11, similar information should be recorded.

Records should be documented separately because they represent a group of closely related data elements. Think of records as rows in a table and each column in the table as an attribute. For example, an applicant would have a row that would contain a column for name, address, education, job titles for which he is qualified, and perhaps an image of the resumé itself.

LOGICAL STRUCTURES AND DECISION TREES

We have discussed models for functional decomposition and data flow and we have detailed the inputs for a data dictionary. Using these models and data dictionary detail, the designer can organize and manage the development of a logical database during the *analysis* phase and early *design* phase. But before discussing Entity Relationship Diagrams (ERDs) in Chapter 2, there is the need to address the logic that is required in the database. Decisions are made during the processing of data. For example, in Figure 1.12, the applicant will be processed differently if he or she is qualified for a position within the company. To assure ourselves that we have the necessary logic in our database, we need to create logical structures and decision trees.

The same results can be achieved using logical or control structures. This modular model uses symbols for *sequence elements, iteration elements*, and *selection elements*. Control structures differ from decision trees in that the process and decisions are controlled. For example, if a condition is not true, one can control that validation or test by re-running it until it becomes true. Figure 1.13 reveals that a test to determine if resumés have run out will run with each resumé sorted until there are no more resumés. At that point, new resumés will be solicited. This is an example

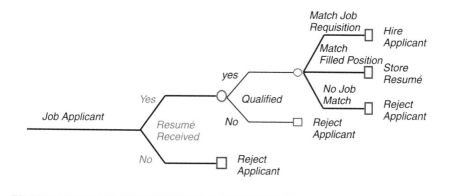

Figure 1.12   Decision tree.

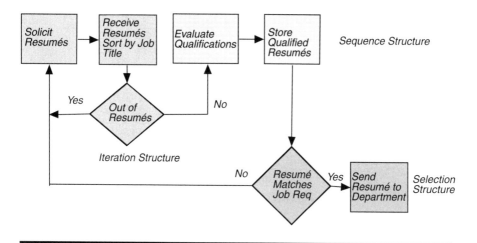

Figure 1.13   Logic or control objects.

of an iteration structure. In the same figure, note that there is also a selection structure. If the test to match a resumé with a job requisition is true, the resumé will be forwarded to the requesting department. Finally, the sequence structure is represented by the steps of evaluating and storing qualified resumés.

SYSTEM DESIGN: LOGICAL

Moving from the *analysis* phase to the *systems design* phase is not an abrupt stop and start of activity; it is more like the blending of activities. Individual or modular processes and data needs identified in the *analysis* phase become more integrated and system-level processes begin to emerge. Critical thinking and analysis come to the forefront. Complex tasks are structured and a prototype database begins to evolve.

We have learned how to model the many modules in our logical database and to use these models to verify with management, users, and systems personnel that we have identified the processes and data requirements of the enterprise. Having established a baseline of existing requirements, we eliminated redundancies and inefficiencies. Our investigations, interviews, and questionnaires have identified the enhancements desired and we understand the logic necessary to incorporate them into our logical database. The next step involves integrating the pieces into a system design and building the prototype database.

The next chapter takes a look at Entity Relation Diagrams (ERDs) and other techniques that will aid the system design process and take us into our final specification and prototype database development, which is part of the implementation phase.

2

SYSTEM DESIGN AND IMPLEMENTATION

Chapter 1 addressed the *planning* and *analysis* phases of our database design. Included in those phases were data collection, a requirements definition, and modeling of the processes and data flows. We now are ready to integrate the pieces into a system design and implement a prototype database. We use an Entity Relation (ER) approach introduced by Chen to model this phase of our database design.

THE ER APPROACH

In the ER approach, entities are objects or things that an enterprise wants to remember. They can be physical (e.g., individuals, products, or buildings) or logical (e.g., departments, accounts, or ideas). Relationships are the connections between the entities; that is, employees *work* in departments or products are *stocked* in warehouses. An entity relationship is diagrammed in Figure 2.1.

Symbols in an ERD may vary between models but all styles work, so choose the symbols that are most effective for you and your organization. Entities in our ER approach have characteristics that must be understood before creating an entity relation diagram (ERD) to model our data and processes.

Knowing how to *create* an ERD includes knowing how to *read* an ERD. At this stage of modeling, we do not have sufficient information about the relationships between the entities in Figure 2.1 to read the diagram correctly. For example, we do not know whether to read the relationship as "Many employees work in a department" or "Many employees work in many departments." What we do know at this stage of modeling is that there is a relationship between the entities and that relationship is a two-way relationship.

Figure 2.1 Entities and relationships.

That is, we would read the ERD first by describing the relationship of employees to departments and then describe the relationship of departments to employees. One might be asking, "Isn't that the same thing?" and the answer would be no. For example, a department might have multiple employees and an employee might have zero or many departments. The relationships that reflect a company's business rules must be incorporated in the ERD. What is important to remember at this stage is that a relationship between two entities is read in both directions to fully describe the relationship.

In beginning to diagram the ER approach, we introduce concepts, working from simple to complex. For example, Figure 2.1 does not address cardinality (i.e., one-to-many relationships), integrity constraints that place restrictions on the entities and/or relationships (i.e., only people with accounting backgrounds can work in the payroll department), or the efficiency of executing queries against our logical database. Each of these topics is addressed as we expand our understanding of the ER approach.

ENTITIES AND ENTITY TYPES

In the example above, Employee is an entity class that contains entities (e.g., John, Terry, and Jeff) about which the business wants to know information. When we examine the Employee class more closely, we see that these entities are limited to those who are employed by the company. A business may want to remember information about other individuals that are not employees (i.e., customers, clients, vendors, etc.). Therefore, the entity class called Employee is really a subset or entity type to the more universal entity type called Individual. The universal entity type is sometimes referred to as a supertype. We can continue our classification process and build a hierarchy of subtypes and supertypes that identifies a particular individual (John) as a technical employee and Terry as an administrative employee.

Figure 2.2 reveals a hierarchy in which John and Terry could be entities that belong to the entity subtype "Technical" and "Administrative," respectively, and that entity type Employee belongs to the supertype Individual. Each entity type would have unique characteristics or attributes that

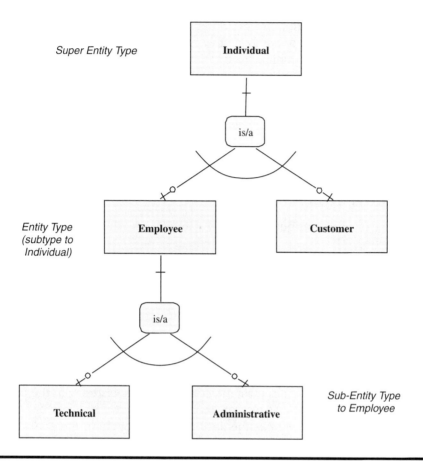

Figure 2.2   Superclass and subclass entities.

distinguish them from other entity types. Another way to think at this hierarchy is to think of each classification as a subtype constraint. That is, John could not belong to the Technical sub-entity unless he possessed the unique characteristics of that entity. To be in the Technical sub-entity, John would have to possess a technical skill such as computer literacy. In the ER approach, these characteristics are called *attributes*.

There are some new symbols in Figure 2.2 that need some explanation. You should already recognize the rectangle as an entity class that contains entities. Each entity in the entity class is represented by a row of data often referred to as a record. The record identifies common attributes of an entity that a business wants to remember. The circle or zero and the bar on the relationship line provide us with information about the cardinality of the relationship. We address cardinality in more detail later in the chapter. The "is/a" block replaces the diamond shape normally used for relationships. It differs from the diamond shape used for relationships because it represents a number of constraints associated with an entity type. Entity type hierarchies are excellent models for conceptual organization and character (attribute) inheritance. They also help us with physical data partitioning—especially when a common database exists in distributed environments. Data partitioning involves assigning fragments of the common database to the location in a network from which most transactions that use that data originate. This saves network access time and is more efficient.

ATTRIBUTE DOMAINS

The domain of an attribute is a set of values from which the attribute can be specified. That is, an attribute's domain is the set of legal or expected values for that attribute. If we identify a gender attribute for the employee entity type, the domain of that attribute would be (male, female).

ATTRIBUTES

Attributes constitute the properties or characteristics of an entity or relationship. The "Individual" entity in Figure 2.2 has certain characteristics that the company would like to remember about each member of that entity. These characteristics form a record that is associated with the entity. For example, John is the name of one member.

Figure 2.3 better identifies the attributes of an entity in the entity class Individual. The attribute SSN is a primary key, as indicated by underline of that attribute. We discuss primary keys more when discussing constraints. For the moment, remember that a primary key is the unique attribute that distinguishes one record in the entity type from another. For every individual (record or entity) in the entity class, the company may want to remember their SSN, Name, Address, and Hobby. These attributes can be stored as single or multiple columns in a table. They can also be stored as classes in an object-oriented database design. The symbols are relatively intuitive so that we know the attribute Address has two sub-attributes or members of a class called Street and City. The symbol for Hobby depicts a set-valued attribute, which means that a record can have more than one hobby.

SET-VALUED ATTRIBUTES

Set-valued attributes will require special attention when translating the ERD into a logical relational database. Although the values fishing, hunting,

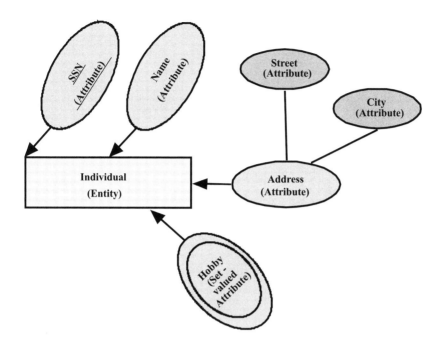

Figure 2.3   Attributes and attribute types.

chess, photography, and hockey are in the same domain, a set-valued attribute means that the entity can have more than one value in the set. This possibility conflicts with relational models, which can contain only sets of entities — not sets of attributes. Confused? Do not be. First understand that "sets of entities" means row or records associated with an entity in an entity class. Then, each row must be distinguished from other rows by a unique attribute (i.e., SSN). If we were to query a database for records with a particular SSN, we might return an instance that contained entities with more than one row because an entity might have more than one hobby. Table 2.1 is a sample of an instance that returns a set of values from a query.

Notice that the instance in Table 2.1 returns three sets of entities (John, Terry, and Jeff). However, the entity John appears twice because John has two hobbies. The primary key did not return a unique record. That is, if we query a relational database for SSN 123-45-6789, more than one record (row) will be returned for the entity 123-45-6789.

Because a relational model requires each record (row) to be unique, we would have to include the hobby in the primary key to form a composite

Table 2.1   Instance with Set-Valued Attributes

Individual			
SSN	Name	Address	Hobby
123-45-6789	John	123 Main Street	Fishing
123-45-6789	John	123 Main Street	Hunting
234-56-7890	Terry	456 Bay Avenue	Chess
234-56-7890	Terry	456 Bay Avenue	Photography
345-67-8901	Jeff	789 Tampa Rd	Hockey

primary key of both SSN and Hobby. This appears to solve the problem because each record is now unique using the composite primary key of (SSN, Hobby). However, we do not need the Hobby attribute to uniquely identify the Name and Address of other records. We are not using the whole key for every record and, worse yet, there is redundant data (Name and Address) being stored. That is, we are not normalized. Although normalization is discussed in detail in Chapter 4, it is helpful to know that multiple values for a single attribute indicate the need for another entity class.

WEAK ENTITIES

In our example, we would convert the attribute Hobby into an entity class. The degree of the relationship (cardinality) between Individual and Hobby would be a many-to-many or an M:N relationship. An individual can have 0 or many hobbies, and hobbies can be enjoyed by 0 or many employees. A relational model with an M:N relationship between two entities can be resolved by creating a weak entity (Hobby Listing) between the two entities (Hobby and Individual).

A weak entity class is one that has no values of its own. In Figure 2.4, SSN and Hobby # are the primary keys of the two strong entities with the M:N relationship.

Referring to Figure 2.3, notice that attributes are common to the entity. That is, SSN, Name, Address, and Hobby are common attributes to the entity Individual. It would not make sense to add an attribute for Spice because individuals do not normally have spices. The concept of limiting attributes for an entity to those attributes that are common to the entity is logical. However, there will be times when an organization wants to remember some information about an entity that is not common to the entity. To do this, the relational model uses foreign key constraints.

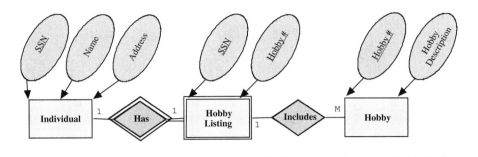

Figure 2.4   Associative (weak) entity.

CONSTRAINTS

There are several constraint types that come into play in a relational model, some more important than others. Constraints are rules restricting what data can be stored or retrieved from a database. Therefore, as a general guideline, constraints should be added after a logical data model is stable. Specifically wait until the model accurately reflects what an enterprise wants to remember and the instances or values stored or retrieved meet user, manager, and IT expectations. Because rules and constraints developed during design frequently change or become obsolete as the data model evolves, limit constraints to those that are universal and unlikely to change. Primary and, to some extent, foreign key constraints fit this definition. Primary key constraints already entered our discussion when we talked about attributes, so let us start with them. They are critical components of a relational database.

Key Constraints: Primary

A primary key consists of one or more attributes of an entity that distinguishes each record from the others. In Figures 2.3 and 2.5, the primary key candidate is the attribute SSN. In Figure 2.3, the attribute SSN did not return a single entity (row) because of the multiple values of the attribute Hobby. We had to create a composite or compound primary key that used two attributes — SSN and Hobby. Looking back at Table 2.1, one can see that if using a composite primary key (SSN, Hobby), each row would be unique. In Figure 2.4, where we normalized the data, SSN by itself will return a single entity (row). Sometimes, finding a unique attribute is difficult or cumbersome. When this occurs, database designers often use sequence numbers such as 1, 2, 3, etc. Notice in Figure 2.4 that Hobby # could be a sequential number. It is an arbitrary attribute created by the designer so that a unique value would exist for each entity in the entity

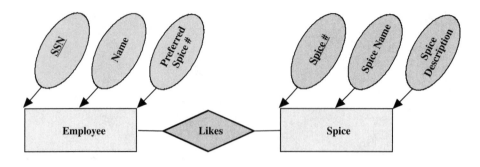

Figure 2.5 Employee and Spice entities.

class Hobby. In addition to being unique, a primary key cannot be null. There must be a value for the attribute every time. Another characteristic is that primary keys are indexed. This allows data to be sorted and retrieved faster. Think of an index as one you would find in a textbook. It has two fields. First we would look up a topic in our textbook index and there we would find a pointer that directed us to particular page in the textbook. In a relational database, we would again find two fields; the first contains the primary or ordering key and the second contains a pointer to a disk block or block address. A relational database example would be: SSN 123-45-6789 in field 1 and an address of block one in the second field. The difference is that the computer uses the block address to find the desired data on the storage disk. You can see the efficiency of an index by comparing the time it would take to search an entire textbook page by page versus using the index and then turning directly to the desired page. All primary keys (attributes) are indexed. Other fields can also be indexed but such fields should be limited to those that are frequently searched, return 2 to 4 percent of the total rows in the database, and where the values differ. It would not be useful to index a field if there are only four records or all the data is the same (e.g., gender would return only male or female).

Key Constraints: Foreign

Foreign keys are used by relational databases to relate entities in one entity class to entities in another entity class. Foreign keys replace pointers and ensure referential integrity. Suppose that a company collects data about an employee. Personal data might be stored in an entity class called Employee. Business data might be stored in an entity type called Department. The two entity types would be related by having common values stored in each entity. We would take the primary key of the Department entity class and add it to the Employee entity class as a foreign key. We can now retrieve all the Department data that is related to a particular employee because the Employee entity (record) contains the Department entity's primary key. Another benefit of foreign keys is referential integrity. If you attempted to store information about an employee in the Employee entity, and entered a department number that did not exist in the Department entity, the database management system (DBMS) would raise an error. That is, you could not assign a foreign key to the Employee entity unless it already existed as a primary key in a Department entity.

From the discussion of attributes, recall that attributes should be common to an entity class. The example used was SSN, Name, Address, and Hobby as common attributes to the entity Individual. We indicated that it would not make sense to add an attribute for Spice because individuals do not normally have spices. But suppose we are a food company and want to know the spice preferences of our employees. To accomplish that, we would use two entity classes: Employee and Spice. In Figure 2.5 we added an attribute for spice preference to the Employee entity class, and created a Spice entity class that would identify all the attributes of spices that the company wanted to remember. The preferred spice number can then be used to create a relationship between the entities. Using this relationship, we can query the database and determine each employee's spice preference.

Storing information as logical entities and relating them by attributes allows an organization to remember information by entity types (Employee and Spice), not the entities themselves. To further explain, try to imagine storing everything you wanted to know about a single entity (John) in an entity class called Employee. The entity John would be a single record that contains an infinite amount of data. Retrieving the data would be simple enough; we would just select "John" from the Employee table in the database. However, efficiency and performance would be adversely affected. Much of the data stored for John would also be stored for other entities such as "Terry" or "Jeff." The relational database approach of storing data by entity types allows us to associate attributes to the entity type and not the entities (John, Mary, or Paul) themselves. SSN, Name, and Preferred Spice would apply to all the entities within the entity type Employee.

LOOKUP TABLES AND CONSISTENCY

When a foreign key exists in a table, the foreign key's table can be referred to as a lookup table. The Department table in our example is a lookup table for the Employee table. That is, the value of an employee's department can be looked up in the Department table. This is an important feature of several relational database management systems (RDBMSs). In

Oracle, for example, one can create a form that allows a user to pick the foreign key data (e.g., Department data) via a lookup table. This option ensures that only valid data is entered in the database because the user is limited to valid departments listed in the lookup table.

Relational database management systems such as Oracle also allow one to link more than one table and they maintain consistency between the tables. Consistency prevents a user from deleting a table when values of that table are being used. That is, the user would not be able to delete a Department that has Employees in it.

MODELING APPROACHES

Thus far, we have defined most of the components of an ER approach. We have addressed entity types, including super- and subtypes, entities or the items contained in an entity type that we want to remember, attributes or the characteristics of the entity that form a record, and finally, constraints or rules that restrict what data can be stored or retrieved. The remaining components are cardinality and relationships. However, before discussing these topics, let us examine our modeling diagrams.

In Figure 2.6, the symbols used in ER Model A illustrate an entity type called Employee with three attributes: SSN, Name, and Preferred Spice #. The SSN attribute is the primary key. Now compare the ER Model A with the Database Table B. Notice that the table name matches the entity type name and the column names match the attributes. The SSN column will be the primary key. In the syntax of a database structure, the primary key is made up of one or more columns in a table that distinguish each row from the others. It is important to see the similarity because we will build our database from the final ERD that is created.

In Figure 2.6, the ER diagram A lends itself to pencil and paper. It is a conceptual model that is easy to draw and supports the interview and informal collection processes in the *analysis* phase.

However, as information about relationships and cardinality is added, ER diagrams like Model A become unwieldy. During the *design* phase, as we finalize our model and add relationships and cardinality, the ER diagram C (which has the same information as Model A and relates well to the database table structure B) is a logical data model and is better at defining the structure of the database. Placing attributes inside the entity box simplifies the model and provides more clarity for relationships.

RELATIONSHIPS

We have stated that every record or entity in an entity class must be distinguished from other records by a primary key. We have also indicated

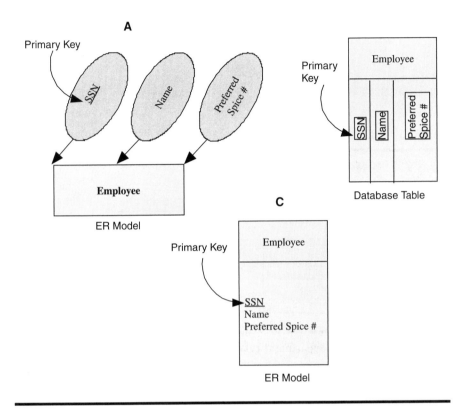

Figure 2.6   Primary keys in ER models and table.

that foreign keys can be used to create relationships between entity classes. Now let us examine how we can use these key constraints to design a relational model.

During the *analysis* phase, we determine that the enterprise would like to remember an employee's social security number; first, middle, and last names; department number; department name; and a description of the functions performed by the department. During the *design* phase, we determine that common attributes can be stored in two entity classes — Employee and Department. Next we create a relationship between the two entity classes by placing the primary key attribute of the Department entity class in the Employee entity class as a foreign key.

Notice in Figure 2.7 that the two entity classes are joined by a horizontal line that represents the relationship. Notice also that the relationship does not include a diamond shape between the entity classes as did the relationship in Figure 2.5. Instead, we see new symbols that represent the degree of the relationship, often referred to as cardinality. The attributes that make up the relationship do not have to have the same names (e.g.,

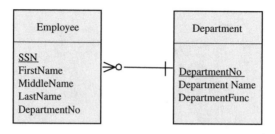

Figure 2.7   Employee and Department ERD.

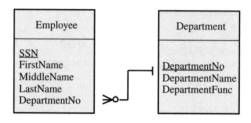

Figure 2.8   Employee/department relationship with foreign key reference.

Listing 2.1   Schema Definitions

```
EMPLOYEE (SSN string, FirstName string, MiddleName string,
         LastName string, DepartmentNo number references
         DEPARTMENT)

DEPARTMENT (DepartmentNo number, DepartmentName string,
            DepartmentFunc string)
```

DepartmentNo in the Employee entity class could be labeled Department-ID or Deptno in the Department entity class). The designer only has to be sure that the data types of the attributes are identical and the values in the field are common to both. However, if the names are different, how can you determine the foreign key from the model?

This can be accomplished by drawing the relationship to reflect the foreign key as drawn in Figure 2.8 or by referring to the schema definitions in Listing 2.1 that supplement the graphical model.

Schema definitions identify the entity class, the attributes in the class, and the data type of each attribute. Do not be intimidated by all the different models and diagramming techniques. As your logical data model evolves, you will probably use a combination of approaches. Summary-

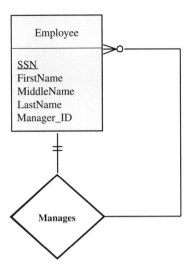

Figure 2.9   Recursive or unary relationship.

level ERDs may exclude the attributes and degree of relationship (cardinality), while detail ERDs may contain the attributes and cardinality and working or implementation ERDs would include attributes, relationships, and definition listings.

What you want to keep in mind is that the graphical models and lists will be used to communicate with users, managers, and designers during the system development life cycle (SDLC). They will also become the backbone of your documentation of the database design.

One relationship not yet discussed is the unary or recursive relationship. This relationship is like joining one table to itself. Figure 2.9 shows the Employee entity class with a recursive foreign key. The data in SSN and Manager_ID is common data. Think of SSN and Manager_ID as being an employee number. An employee must have one and only one manager and a manager can supervise zero or many employees.

CARDINALITY

Using the model in Figure 2.7, we can determine information about the entity class and the relationships between Employee and Department based on the symbols used. For example, a bar appears inside the Employee box and separates the entity class title from the attributes. When we see a partitioning bar inside a box, as in Figure 2.7, we know that the enterprise wants to remember the following about its employees: SSN, First Name, Middle Name, Last Name, and Department No. Because there is an underline of the attribute SSN inside the box, we know two more

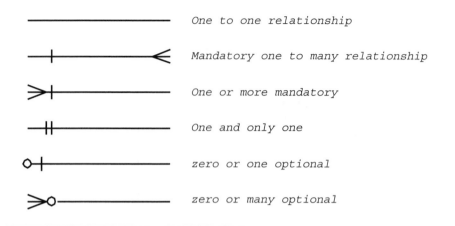

Figure 2.10 Relationship symbols.

things about the entity class: (1) the enterprise must remember the employee's SSN and (2) no two employees can have the same SSN.

Now notice the vertical bar on the relationship line closest to the entity class Department in Figure 2.7. This bar means that an employee must be associated with one department. Also notice the crow's feet and zero near the employee entity class. This means a department may have zero or many employees. Other relationship symbols are pictured in Figure 2.10.

Cardinality has to do with the degree of a relationship. The relationship of entities between entity classes may be one to one, one to many, or zero to many. Relationships between entities are bi-directional. That is, an employee must be in one department and departments may have zero or many employees.

As an illustration, we can use the matrices in Tables 2.2 and 2.3 to define instances of the Employee and Department tables, respectively. In the Employee table, the columns (attributes) are labeled SSN, First Name, Middle Name, Last Name, and Department No. The rows are an instance showing the value for each entity or record in the table.

The instance of the Employee table in Table 2.2 has four records representing four employees. The primary key is the SSN and it serves several purposes. It is unique, it cannot be null, and it is indexed. The Department No. is the foreign key constraint that references the Department table and creates a relationship. Notice the correlation between the ERD in Figure 2.7 and the table instance in Table 2.2.

In the Department table, the columns (attributes) are labeled Department No., Department Name, and Department Function. The rows are an instance showing the value for each entity or record in the table. The Department table in Table 2.3 has four records representing four departments. The primary key is the Department No. Notice how the primary

Table 2.2   Employee Table

Employee Table				
SSN	First Name	Middle Name	Last Name	Department No.
123-45-6789	Tim	L.	Smith	001
234-56-7890	Jane	M.	Doe	002
345-67-8901	Jane	M.	Brown	003
456-78-9012	Tim	L.	Smith jr.	002

Table 2.3   Department Table

Department Table		
Department No	Department Name	Department Function
001	Admin.	Clerical and administrative activities (excludes management)
002	Sales	Product sales
003	Operations	Product manufacturing
004	Management	Executives and managers

key is used in the Employee entity (Figure 2.7) and the Employee instance (Table 2.2) to link the entity data together between the two tables.

As part of the SDLC, we always want to test our design to be sure that it returns the data the enterprise wants to remember. Table instances serve this purpose. They assure designers that the relational models being created accurately reflect an enterprise's requirements.

If we attempt to add an employee to our database and place him in Department No. 900, the RDBMS would display an error because Department 900 does not exist in the Department table. That is, we would have referential integrity because we used a foreign key constraint. The RDBMS would not allow us to corrupt our database and refer to a department that does not exist.

SCHEMAS

We have used the term "schema definitions" and now might be a good time to define schema. In the broadest sense, a schema is a specification of the physical database's information content and logical structure. The structure could be the overall database or an object inside the database. A table's structure would be considered a schema because it defines the structure in terms of its columns or attributes. (Note: The rows in a table would be considered an instance.) A logical data model is like a schema because it is a description of what kind of information will go into a database and how that information will be structured or organized. If you are already a designer, you might be thinking that you have a personal schema, and you would be correct. Users have different requirements and therefore each different kind of user must be provided with a schema that is specific to his or her requirements.

IMPLEMENTATION: CONVERTING THE ERD

To convert our ERD into a logical database design, we need only to review the topics discussed in this chapter and organize them into steps:

1. Create relation schemas for all the strong entities. This means creating a schema definition similar to that in Listing 2.1. The entity class will become the name of the relation schema. The single-value attributes will become attributes in the relation schema with the primary key designated by an underline.
2. Break down composite attributes like those in Figure 2.3 (city, street) into their components and add them individually to the relation schema.
3. Break out multi-valued attributes into a new relation schema. Because the degree of this relationship may be many to many, a weak entity between the two relation schemas might be required as in Figure 2.4.
4. Map the cardinality of the relationships 1:1 and 1:M by adding foreign keys to the appropriate relation schema. In a 1:1 relation, the foreign key can go in either schema. The designer must logically choose the appropriate relation. As an alternative, a 1:1 relation schema can be condensed into a single entity. In a 1:M relation, the foreign key would go in the Many relation schema.
5. Map unary relationships. These are recursive relationships in a single entity class between instances or rows similar to that in Figure 2.9. A sample relation schema is depicted in Listing 2.2. Finally, map the inherited attributes (superclass entities and subclass entities similar to those in Figure 2.2). Although superclass entities and subclass entities are not directly supported by relational databases,

Listing 2.2 Inherited Attribute

```
EMPLOYEE (SSN, FirstName, MiddleName, LastName, Manager_ID)
```

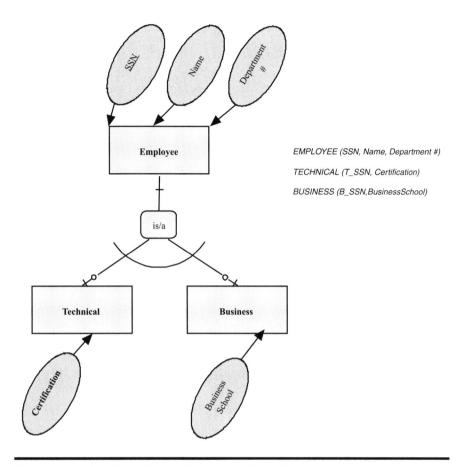

Figure 2.11   Relation schemas for inherited attributes.

there is a work-around. First create a separate relation schema for each super/subclass entity. Next, assign all common attributes to the super-relation schema and the unique attributes to their respective relation schema. Finally, add the super-relation primary key to each of the sub-relation schemas. It is helpful to rename the primary key in the sub-relation schemas to reflect the distinguishing characteristic of the sub-relation. The result can be seen in Figure 2.11.

Although we did not discuss derived attributes, you will probably use some in your data model. These derived attributes are calculated in the database and not supported in a relational database. Therefore they will not appear in a relation schema.

SPECIFICATIONS AND DOCUMENTATION

The models and schema relations that you will create in the *analysis, design,* and *implementation* phases form the cornerstone of your documentation and specifications. Broadly speaking, documentation will fall into two general categories: user and system.

User documentation includes written procedures, tutorials, training, and help references. They may be in written form with graphical illustrations, stored online with the application, organized on an intranet or the Internet with streaming video, or placed on CDs or DVDs. The media should be the most convenient for the user and geared toward the users' needs. That is, the documentation should be layered. More technical detail should be limited to super-users with technical knowledge, while summarized documentation on a conceptual level should be available for management. The documentation should tell the user how it works and how to use it.

System documentation is the detailed information about a system's design, processes, and functionality. Included would be the requirements specifications, architectural design, prototype and production designs, test specifications, and test results during implementation. System documentation can further be refined into internal and external categories. Internal documentation would include the models and diagrams discussed. It includes source code and documentation generated at compile time. External documentation would include the outcomes or results of the internal processes and procedures.

The data dictionary is an RDBMS methodology for storing definitions of database objects. These definitions are retained in the database and can be retrieved by anyone granted the system privilege to access data dictionary views. Packages, procedures, functions, and triggers can be stored on the database. Object definitions and code stored on the relational database should be commented and documented.

From these descriptions, the task of documenting the system is daunting. There will be extraordinary pressure to release the system to production before documentation is complete or, worse, without adequate documentation. As the designer, you must persuade managers and others in the company regarding the importance of proper documentation. Without it, maintenance and troubleshooting will be substantially more difficult and costly. Also, designers familiar with the system will forget important details as time elapses and designers may be lost to other projects or companies.

Documentation (particularly the models and relation schemas) can be used to create tables and relationships when we build our database. Chapter 3 introduces the techniques and language to do this.

3

CONVERTING THE LOGICAL DATA MODEL

Chapter 1 introduced the system development life cycle (SDLC) in Figure 1.4 (duplicated here as Figure 3.1). We learned how to use analytical and interpersonal skills to identify an enterprise's requirements by gathering information through interviews, questionnaires, meetings, and document reviews. We learned how to translate those requirements into a relational data model using checklists, functional decomposition diagrams (FDDs), data flow diagrams (DFDs), logical structures, and decision trees. We learned how to document the structure and detail associated with these models in a data dictionary.

In Chapter 2 we learned how to take the requirements identified in the *requirements* phase of the SDLC and create a logical design using the ER approach. We learned how to create an ERD by diagramming entities types, entities, attributes, relationships, and cardinality in the *logical design* phase of the SDLC. In the *specification* phase, we learned how to create a specification by documenting the final ERD and creating logical schema listings.

DATABASE ARCHITECTURE

In this chapter, we want learn how to implement a prototype database with schemas and instances to test our logical data model. To accomplish this task we need to find an approach that is transparent to the environment in which our database will reside. The environment includes several elements: (1) hardware — mainframe or distributed systems; (2) operating systems — UNIX, Linux, or Windows; and (3) a relational database management system — IBM, Microsoft, Oracle, or Sybase.

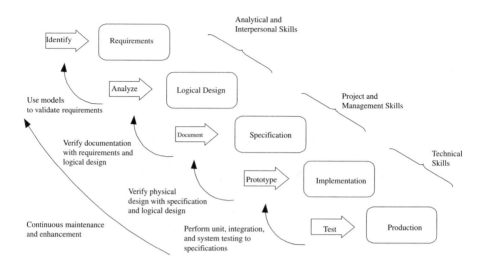

Figure 3.1   System development life cycle (SDLC).

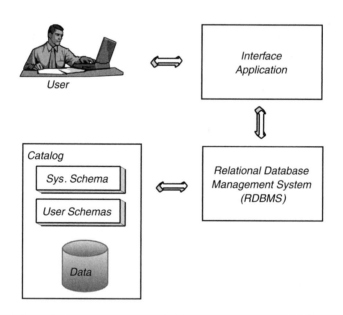

Figure 3.2   Logical and physical environment.

For example, Figure 3.2 could represent a user on a distributed computer system using a Windows operating system and a custom-designed application that interfaces with an Oracle RDBMS to manage the relational database that we designed using our logical data model.

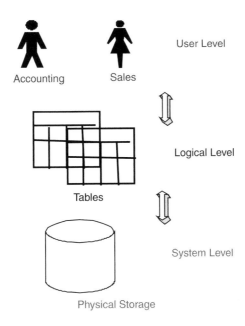

Figure 3.3   Schema levels.

Although the elements of the environment are critical to the physical design and implementation, we can build and interface with our relational database on a logical level. We can create schemas and instances that will be stored in the database. A schema, if you recall from Chapter 2, is a database's structure and an instance is the content or values stored in that database.

It may help to understand the different types or levels of schemas. A database has three schema levels: (1) a system level, (2) a logical level, and (3) a user level. The user level represents distinct views that are customized to the needs of the individual users. For example, users in the accounting department would have a view of the database that included the salaries of employees, while users in the sales department would have views of sales figures and inventory. The logical level would be a collection of table schemas such as an employee table and a department table, each with attributes as columns. This level would include mappings to the user schemas. The system level is a collection of software and file schemas (see Figure 3.3).

This level would include mappings to the logical level. Schema levels make it possible for users, developers, and database administrators to work within their level without having to know anything about the other levels. To work within varied environments at the logical level requires a Structured Query Language (SQL) that can convert our data model into a database.

SQL

Chapter 1 discussed E. F. Codd's contribution to relational database theory. In 1970, Codd's theories were tested by engineers at IBM Research Laboratories to demonstrate the feasibility of creating a database management system for a relational model. The engineers used a language originally referred to as SEQUEL (Structured English QUEry Language) but later shortened to SQL. This language has become the *de facto* standard used by developers to create and manage relational databases. As the language evolved, it was accepted by the American National Standards Institute (ANSI) and is a Federal Information Processing Standard (FIPS). Internationally, it is recognized by the International Standards Organization (ISO).

The benefits of a structured language like SQL are standardized coding conventions and its simplicity for users. The user does not have to learn machine language or even a 4GL language, and the number of commands to learn is very manageable. Table 3.1 categorizes SQL commands into meaningful groups and describes the category's functionality.

DDL COMMANDS

Because we are building a prototype relational database, we will begin with DDL commands of SQL to convert our data model. Recall that at the logical level of schemas, tables are structures used to store data. Our first example will be the schema definition in Listing 3.1.

We begin by using the SQL CREATE command. The syntax for creating the EMPLOYEE table schema appears in Listing 3.2. (Note: Coding examples will use an Oracle environment called SQL* Plus. This environment has its own commands, but that is another book.) The syntax is the same between RDBMSs as long as we restrict our commands to the ANSI standard. Some syntax differences might be the declaration of the data type. Oracle uses Varchar2 for a variable string, while other RDBMSs might use a different descriptor.

The CREATE command tells the RDBMS to create an object; the next word "table" tells the RDBMS what type of object to create. Inside the parentheses, the attributes of the data model are converted into columns in the table. Notice that each attribute also defines the data type of the attribute. Defining the attribute helps the RDBMS maintain data integrity. That is, if you attempt to store data that is of a different data type, an error will be raised. Finally, the number that appears in parentheses after a data type refers to its size. For example, the SSN is a variable string data type that may be up to 13 characters in length.

Table 3.1 SQL Command

SQL Commands	Category	Purpose
SELECT	Data retrieval	Retrieve data from the database
INSERT UPDATE DELETE MERGE	Data Manipulation Language (DML) Note: DML commands need implicit or explicit DCL statement to confirm/save or undo a transaction (group of DML statements)	Enters new data, changes data, or removes data in a single row of a table
CREATE ALTER DROP RENAME TRUNCATE	Data Definition Language (DDL) Note: Includes an implicit confirmation/ commit TC statement	Defines structures within the database, creating, changing removing, or renaming schema objects
COMMIT ROLLBACK SAVEPOINT	Transactional Control (TC)	DML actions can be confirmed or undone as single statements or groups of statements (called transactions)
GRANT REVOKE	Data Control Language (DCL)	Assigns or removes access rights to the system or objects

Listing 3.1 Employee Schema Definition

```
EMPLOYEE (SSN string, FirstName string, MiddleName string,
          LastName string, DepartmentNo number references
          DEPARTMENT)
```

Listing 3.2 Syntax for Creating Table Schema

```
Create table EMPLOYEE
(SSN            Varchar2(13),
 FirstName      Varchar2(10),
 MiddleName     Varchar2(10),
 LastName       Varchar2(10),
 DepartmentNo   Number);
```

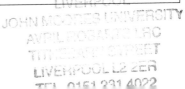

Listing 3.3   Schema or Structure of EMPLOYEE Table

```
SQL> SELECT TABLE_NAME, COLUMN_NAME, DATA_TYPE, DATA_LENGTH,
NULLABLE
  2  FROM USER_TAB_COLUMNS
  3  WHERE TABLE_NAME = 'EMPLOYEE';

TABLE_NAME    COLUMN_NAME      DATA_TYPE      DATA_LENGTH NULLABLE
------------  ---------------  -------------  ----------- --------
EMPLOYEE      SSN              VARCHAR2                13 Y
EMPLOYEE      FIRSTNAME        VARCHAR2                10 Y
EMPLOYEE      MIDDLENAME       VARCHAR2                10 Y
EMPLOYEE      LASTNAME         VARCHAR2                10 Y
EMPLOYEE      DEPARTMENTNO     NUMBER                  22 Y
```

It is important to understand that the table definition in Listing 3.2 is stored in the database in the data dictionary. You can query the many views in the data dictionary whenever you want to see the structure of an object defined in the database. Note: To query the data dictionary views, you will have to be granted the appropriate system access privileges. Listing 3.3 is a sample of a data dictionary query that returns the EMPLOYEE table structure.

We will review the syntax for queries later. For the moment, you can see from Listing 3.3 that our CREATE statement in Listing 3.2 defined the EMPLOYEE table and stored it in the database. The information in the database tells us that the table's structure consists of five columns and identifies their respective data types. When you look at the Data_Length field for DepartmentNo, you see it is 22, which is the default value for data type Number when no size or precision is defined. The last column tells us that all columns may have a null value.

Recalling Chapter 2 discussions regarding entities and constraints, the SSN number should have a Not Null constraint because it is the attribute designated as the primary key in the Listing 3.2 schema definition. Before we correct the shortcoming, we take this opportunity to emphasize the importance of documentation. A major goal of our prototype database is to validate our design and verify that all components are incorporated. Once these goals are achieved, the next goal is to verify that the query results satisfy the needs of the organization. None of these goals can be achieved if they are not documented before we convert our data model into a prototype database.

The primary key can be included in the CREATE statement (Listing 3.5) or added later by modifying the table with the ALTER command. To reissue the CREATE statement, we would have to first DROP the table object (Listing 3.4). In Listing 3.5, we designate the SSN column as the table's primary key (see Listing 3.6). We also name the constraint

Listing 3.4 DROP Command

```
SQL> DROP table EMPLOYEE;

Table dropped.
```

Listing 3.5 Syntax for Creating Table Schema with Primary Key Constraint

```
Create table EMPLOYEE
(SSN          Varchar2(13) CONSTRAINT PK_Employee primary key,
 FirstName    Varchar2(10),
 MiddleName   Varchar2(10),
 LastName     Varchar2(10),
 DepartmentNo Number);
```

Listing 3.6 Constraint Definition Stored in Database

```
SQL> select table_name, constraint_name, constraint_type
  2  from user_constraints
  3  where table_name = 'EMPLOYEE';

TABLE_NAME    CONSTRAINT_NAME                      CONSTRAINT_TYPE
------------  ----------------------------  -
EMPLOYEE      PK_EMPLOYEE                          P
```

PK_Employee. Naming a constraint is not required when using the Oracle RDBMS because Oracle will assign a distinct name when no name is provided.

However, naming the constraint provides valuable information when validating constraints stored in the data dictionary. If we allow Oracle to name the constraint, it would be difficult to recognize. See the difference in Listing 3.7 when the table is created without naming the primary key constraint. The constraint name SYS_C003219 does not tell us anything about the constraint. It would be helpful to know the constraint type and the table objects with which it is associated. Good naming practices will provide this information.

When you query the data dictionary, you will see that the SSN column has several new characteristics: (1) field values in the column may no longer be null, (2) the field values are indexed, and (3) the field values must be unique. These characteristics can be seen in Listing 3.8, where the data dictionary views for indexes and constraints are queried for the EMPLOYEE table created. We will be able to query these same views to verify other constraints when they are added to the table. Note: Constraints, other than the primary key, are usually added to a table using the ALTER

Listing 3.7   Creating Table Schema with Unnamed Primary Key Constraint

```
SQL> drop table Employee;

Table dropped.

SQL> Create table EMPLOYEE
  2  (SSN            Varchar2(13) primary key,
  3  FirstName      Varchar2(10),
  4  MiddleName     Varchar2(10),
  5  LastName       Varchar2(10),
  6  DepartmentNo Number);

Table created.

SQL> select table_name, constraint_name, constraint_type
  2  from user_constraints
  3  where table_name = 'EMPLOYEE';

TABLE_NAME    CONSTRAINT_NAME                          CONSTRAINT_TYPE
------------  -------------------------------  -
EMPLOYEE      SYS_C003219                              P
```

Listing 3.8   Data Dictionary View of Primary Key Characteristics

```
SQL> SELECT INDEX_NAME, INDEX_TYPE, UNIQUENESS, TABLE_NAME
  2  FROM USER_INDEXES
  3  WHERE TABLE_NAME = 'EMPLOYEE';

INDEX_NAME                INDEX_TYPE              UNIQUENESS TABLE_NAME
----------------------    ----------------------  --------- ----------
PK_EMPLOYEE               NORMAL                  UNIQUE     EMPLOYEE

SQL> SELECT TABLE_NAME, COLUMN_NAME, DATA_TYPE, DATA_LENGTH, NULLABLE
     FROM USER_TAB_COLUMNS
     WHERE TABLE_NAME = 'EMPLOYEE';

TABLE_NAME           COLUMN_NAME       DATA_TYPE     DATA_LENGTH NULLABLE
-------------------- ---------------   ------------  ----------- --------
EMPLOYEE             SSN               VARCHAR2             13 N
EMPLOYEE             FIRSTNAME         VARCHAR2             10 Y
EMPLOYEE             MIDDLENAME        VARCHAR2             10 Y
EMPLOYEE             LASTNAME          VARCHAR2             10 Y
EMPLOYEE             DEPARTMENTNO      NUMBER               22 Y
```

command. Adding constraints after the database structure is complete makes it easier to test individual components of the database without violating constraints. Another approach is to create the constraints and then disable them using the ALTER command before testing. Either approach is acceptable.

Listing 3.9   Dropping and Creating the EMPLOYEE Table

```
SQL> drop table employee;

Table dropped.

SQL> Create table EMPLOYEE
  2   (SSN           Varchar2(13),
  3    FirstName     Varchar2(10),
  4    MiddleName    Varchar2(10),
  5    LastName      Varchar2(10),
  6    DepartmentNo  Number);

Table created.
```

Listing 3.10   Altering the Table and Adding Constraint(s)

```
SQL> ALTER table EMPLOYEE
  2   add
  3   constraint PK_Employee primary key (SSN);

Table altered.

SQL> select table_name, constraint_name, constraint_type
  2   from user_constraints
  3   where table_name = 'EMPLOYEE';

TABLE_NAME    CONSTRAINT_NAME                   C
------------  ------------------------------    -
EMPLOYEE      PK_EMPLOYEE                        P
```

To add constraints to a table after it has been created is done using the ALTER command. In Listing 3.9 we drop the table EMPLOYEE and then recreate it without its primary key.

We then add a primary key (which includes implicit Not Null and Unique constraints, plus an Index) using the ALTER command. A query of the data dictionary will verify the implicit constraints and the index. The results of the query will be identical to the values in Listing 3.10.

In Listing 3.11, a foreign key constraint named FK_Employee_SSN_DeptNo references the DeptNo column in the DEPARTMENT table. (Note: DeptNo is the primary key for the DEPARTMENT table.)

If the designer includes the foreign key in the CREATE statement, he must understand that constraints may make the testing and building of the database cumbersome and difficult. For example, in Listing 3.12 you can see the results when a foreign key is created in a table before the referenced table is created.

Listing 3.11 Including Foreign Key in CREATE Statement

```
Create table EMPLOYEE
(SSN            Varchar2(13) CONSTRAINT PK_Employee primary key,
 FirstName      Varchar2(10),
 MiddleName     Varchar2(10),
 LastName       Varchar2(10),
 DepartmentNo Number       CONSTRAINT FK_Employee_SSN_DeptNo references
                           DEPARTMENT (Deptno));
```

Listing 3.12 Error Creating Foreign Key Constraint

```
SQL> Create table EMPLOYEE
  2 (SSN            Varchar2(13) CONSTRAINT PK_Employee primary key,
  3 FirstName      Varchar2(10),
  4 MiddleName     Varchar2(10),
  5 LastName       Varchar2(10),
  6 DepartmentNo Number       CONSTRAINT FK_Employee_SSN_DeptNo references
  7                           DEPARTMENT (DepartmentNo));

                   Department (departmentNo))
                   *

ERROR at line 7:
ORA-00942: table or view does not exist
```

Listing 3.13 Using ALTER to Add Foreign Key

```
SQL> ALTER table EMPLOYEE
  2   add
  3   CONSTRAINT FK_Employee_SSN_DeptNo Foreign Key(DepartmentNo)
references
      DEPARTMENT (DepartmentNo));

Table altered.
```

When adding a foreign key, the preferred method is to use the ALTER command after the database has stabilized. Listing 3.13 shows the syntax. This approach will avoid referencing tables or views that have not yet been created as well as dropping tables or constraints being referenced by another object.

The remaining DDL commands for SQL include RENAME and TRUNCATE. RENAME is intuitive and allows you to rename objects in the database. For example, Listing 3.14 renames the table EMPLOYEE to EMP9 and then back again. TRUNCATE removes all rows from a table, but differs from the DML command DELETE in two ways: (1) TRUNCATE releases the storage space used by that table, (2) the TRUNCATE command cannot be rolled back while the DML command DELETE can be rolled back. That

Listing 3.14   Renaming an Object

```
SQL> RENAME EMPLOYEE TO EMP9;

Table renamed.

SQL> RENAME EMP9 TO EMPLOYEE;

Table renamed.
```

Listing 3.15   Truncating a Table

```
SQL> select * from EMPLOYEE;

SSN             FIRSTNAME  MIDDLENAME LASTNAME   DEPARTMENTNO
-------------   ---------- ---------- ---------- ------------
123-45-6789     Thomas     J.         Walker            100
123-45-6790     Terry      L.         Toye              101

SQL> TRUNCATE Table EMPLOYEE;

Table truncated.

SQL> select * from EMPLOYEE;

no rows selected
```

is, you do not issue a COMMIT command for DDL commands — it is implicit. You can roll back a DML command if an implicit or explicit COMMIT command has not been issued. The syntax for truncating a table is shown in Listing 3.15.

Before leaving DDL commands, remember that to create objects, constraints, and references requires that these privileges plus connect and session be granted to you.

DATA RETRIEVAL

Many of the figures in this chapter use queries to demonstrate an action taken on the database. To query the database, you will use the SELECT command to create a Select Statement that returns rows from database tables or views (including data dictionary views). Listing 3.15 shows the syntax for retrieving data from a single table. The SELECT command is a required keyword that must start the Select Statement. Following the SELECT keyword is a listing of column names separated by commas. You can list as many columns as you want. Notice that a comma is not placed after the last column in the list. The RDBMS recognizes the missing comma

Listing 3.16   Implicit Cursors

```
SQL> SELECT SSN, FIRSTNAME , LASTNAME LAST_NAME
   2 FROM EMPLOYEE;

SSN             FIRSTNAME   LAST_NAME
-------------   ----------  ----------
123-45-6789     Thomas      Walker
123-45-6790     Terry       Toye
```

and looks for either a column alias or the FROM keyword. An alias is just a way of temporarily renaming a column heading. In Listing 3.16, the alias LAST_NAME is substituted for the column name LASTNAME. An alias does not change the column name in the database, just the display column header.

DML STATEMENTS AND IMPLICIT CURSORS

A SELECT statement is one of the many SQL statements that can be issued to the RDBMS. Figure 3.4 depicts the steps a RDBMS goes through as it interacts with the database. The steps are taken automatically by the RDBMS and are implicit or transparent to the user: DML results in the following steps: (1) The RDBMS first declares and opens a temporary storage area known as a cursor. (2) The statement/code is parsed. This means the syntax is checked for accuracy (keywords and punctuation) and whether database objects are valid. Input variables are bound. The active set is identified using the search criteria of the SELECT statement

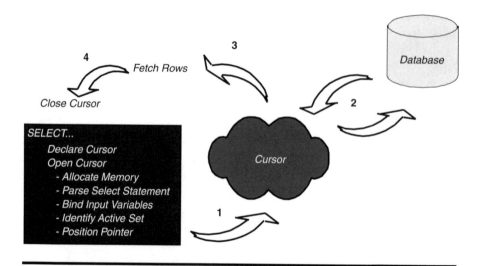

Figure 3.4   SELECT statement.

and stored in the cursor. A pointer is placed above the first row of the active set in the cursor. (3) Rows are fetched from the cursor. (4) The cursor is closed and memory released. You do not have to understand these steps to use SELECT and DML statements but it will help the reader understand how SQL interfaces with the database.

SELECT STATEMENTS

Using the statement in Listing 3.16, the keyword SELECT tells the RDBMS that it will be retrieving data from the database and that a list of desired columns and aliases should appear next in the statement. The RDBMS uses the commas in the list as a delimiter to distinguish one column name and alias from another. In Listing 3.16, there are three columns and one alias. Notice that the column names are separated by a comma. Where a comma does not appear, the RDBMS looks for either an alias or the keyword FROM. Because there is no comma after the column name LastName, and the next word is not FROM, the RDBMS interprets the next word to be an alias. Finding no comma after the alias, the RDBMS looks for the FROM keyword. Having found the anticipated keyword, the RDBMS then looks for a list of tables or views. Again, commas will act as delimiters. This process of walking through an SQL statement is known as parsing. The RDBMS checks for the correct syntax and then verifies that the objects in the statement exist (are defined) in the database. In Figure 3.4, the RDBMS would verify that the table object EMPLOYEE is valid. After parsing the statement, input variables (variables outside the SQL statement or processing language in which an SQL statement can be embedded) are bound and an active set placed in the cursor. Rows are fetched and displayed and the implicit cursor closed. The displayed results or data retrieved show two employees Thomas and Terry.

The only limit on what data can be retrieved from the database is the architecture or structure itself. That is why the data model is so critical and why we test to verify whether data retrieved meets the needs of the enterprise. The SELECT statement can include a number of clauses and Listing 3.17 illustrates them. These clauses are covered in SQL texts and, as a designer, you should study them in detail. They will allow you to display

Listing 3.17   Available SELECT Statement Clauses

```
SELECT      column(s), column column_alias, single_row_function(s),
              group_function(s)
FROM        table, table table_alias, view
WHERE       condition(s)
GROUP BY    group_by_expression(s)
HAVING      group_condition(s)
ORDER BY    column(s)
```

Listing 3.18   Schema Definitions

```
EMPLOYEE (SSN string, FirstName string, MiddleName string,
          LastName string, DepartmentNo number references
          DEPARTMENT)

DEPARTMENT (DepartmentNo number, DepartmentName string,
            DepartmentFunc string)
```

Listing 3.19   Using a Relationship to Join Tables Using a WHERE Clause

```
SQL> SELECT e.FirstName, e.LastName, d.DepartmentName DEPARTMENT
  2  FROM EMPLOYEE e, DEPARTMENT d
  3  WHERE e.DepartmentNo = d.DepartmentNo;

FIRSTNAME   LASTNAME    DEPARTMENT
----------  ----------  ---------------
Thomas      Walker      ADMIN
Terry       Toye        SALES
Fred        Smith       SALES
```

many different instances. Although the SELECT clause and FROM clause are the only required clauses for a SELECT Statement, we will briefly discuss the WHERE clause. This clause is used frequently to limit the number of rows returned for an instance and to join tables in your query. Using the schema definitions in Chapter 2, Listing 2.1, and duplicated here as Listing 3.18, we have created an EMPLOYEE table and a DEPARTMENT table. We then created a relationship and referential integrity between the tables when we altered the EMPLOYEE table and added a foreign key that referenced the DepartmentNo column in the DEPARTMENT table.

We can test our schemas by querying the database. Let us retrieve the names of all our employees and the name of the department in which they work. Listing 3.19 confirms that we have three employees in the company: one in Administration and two in Sales. But how did we get the department name? It is not stored in the EMPLOYEE table. The answer is we had to join two tables: the EMPLOYEE and DEPART-MENT tables. This was possible because we created a relationship between the two table schemas when we defined them in the database. They both share common data — specifically, both tables have a column that stores the department number. Relationships can be used in a query by setting the WHERE clause condition to limit the rows (records) returned from the database to those rows where the DepartmentNo in the EMPLOYEE table matches or equals the DepartmentNo in the DEPARTMENT table. When joining tables, you will need (n–1) joins, where n is the number of tables.

Listing 3.20   WHERE Clause Limits Rows Returned

```
SQL> select e.FirstName, e.LastName, d.DepartmentName DEPARTMENT
  2  from EMPLOYEE e, DEPARTMENT d
  3  WHERE e.DepartmentNo = d.DepartmentNo
  4  AND d.DepartmentName = 'SALES'
  5  Order By e.LastName;


FIRSTNAME   LASTNAME    DEPARTMENT
----------  ----------  ----------------
Fred        Smith       SALES
Terry       Toye        SALES
```

Before moving to another query, some lessons can be learned about the SQL statement in Listing 3.19. The SELECT clause contains a column alias (DEPARTMENT) and references to table aliases ("e." and "d."), sometimes referred to as dot nomenclature. We have already discussed the column alias so let us look at the table aliases used. When the SQL statement is processed by the RDBMS, it searches through all the tables listed in the FROM clause for the columns listed in the SELECT clause. By adding the table aliases, ambiguous column names are avoided and the search is more efficient because all tables do not have to be searched for all columns. Table aliases are assigned in the FROM clause the same way column aliases are added. The RDBMS searches for a list of tables or views after the keyword FROM. Each table is separated by a comma delimiter. Any string that follows a table name and a space without a comma is interpreted to be a table alias.

In Listing 3.20 we have added a second condition to our WHERE clause (line 4) and an Order By clause (line 5). The second WHERE clause condition limits the number of rows returned to those where the DepartmentName matches/equals SALES. Notice that the second WHERE condition begins with an AND. This is a logical operator and means that both conditions must be true for the records returned. Had we used an OR logical operator, then only one of the conditions would have to be true. You can have as many WHERE conditions as you need.

Now the display in Listing 3.20 shows only two records — both are in sales. Notice that the order of the names being displayed is different. It is sorted by LastName because we used an Order By clause to establish the sorting criteria.

CARTESIAN PRODUCT

Before leaving the SELECT statement, it is important to understand what happens when you attempt to query multiple tables without using a table join in the WHERE clause. Notice in Listing 3.21 that nine rows (records)

Listing 3.21 Cartesian Product

```
SQL> select e.firstname, e.lastname, d.departmentname DEPARTMENT
  2  from EMPLOYEE e, DEPARTMENT d
  3  --WHERE e.DepartmentNo = d.DepartmentNo    Lines 3 and 4 are
  4  --AND d.DepartmentName = 'SALES'           commented out
  5  Order By e.LastName;

FIRSTNAME   LASTNAME    DEPARTMENT
----------  ----------  ---------------
Fred        Smith       ADMIN
Fred        Smith       SALES
Fred        Smith       Marketing
Terry       Toye        ADMIN
Terry       Toye        SALES
Terry       Toye        Marketing
Thomas      Walker      ADMIN
Thomas      Walker      SALES
Thomas      Walker      Marketing

9 rows selected.
```

are displayed. Because there is no table join (the '--' symbol comments out the line of code to the right of the double dashes), each record in the EMPLOYEE table is matched with each line in the DEPARTMENT table. Because the EMPLOYEE table has three records and the DEPARTMENT table has three records, one gets nine records displayed ($3 \times 3 = 9$). This is called a Cartesian product.

DML: INSERT COMMANDS

Looking back at Table 3.1 one sees that we have discussed the DDL commands and the SELECT command. Now we look at the DML or Data Manipulation Language commands. These commands are used to manipulate data in the database. They allow you to INSERT new data, UPDATE or change existing data, and DELETE or remove data. You will use DML statements to place data in the database for testing. DML will also allow you to modify data. These capabilities are important because you need to know what values are in the database so that when you run a query, you can predict what should be displayed. Listing 3.22 shows the syntax for adding a record to the EMPLOYEE table. In Line 1, we use the keyword INSERT with a required 'INTO' plus the table name. Line 2 identifies the columns in the table where we want to insert values. Although Line 2 is optional, it is good coding practice to identify the columns to avoid mistakes while entering data. Listing the columns also allows you to insert values for select columns rather than all columns. That is, if you do not

Listing 3.22   INSERT Statement

```
SQL> INSERT into EMPLOYEE
  2   (SSN, FirstName, MiddleName, LastName, DepartmentNo)
  3   Values
  4   ('123-45-6792', 'Joseph', 'David', 'Doe', 102);

1 row created.

SQL> Select *
  2   From EMPLOYEE;

SSN             FIRSTNAME   MIDDLENAME  LASTNAME    DEPARTMENTNO
-------------   ---------   ----------  ----------  ------------
123-45-6789     Thomas      J.          Walker               100
123-45-6790     Terry       L.          Toye                 101
123-45-6791     Fred                    Smith                101
123-45-6792     Joseph      David       Doe                  102

SQL> commit
```

list the columns, you must insert a value or a null for each column. Plus, you must remember the order of the columns. When listing columns in Line 2, do not forget to include parentheses. Line 3 is required and alerts the RDBMS that the values to be inserted are coming next. Line 4 identifies the values to be inserted. The values must match the data type of the column and follow the same order as listed in Line 2. Notice the single quote (' ') marks around the values for SSN, FirstName, MiddleName, and LastName. These indicate that the values are strings and match the data type defined for the column when the table was created. The last value 102 is a number and does not require quote marks. Before leaving Listing 3.21, notice the SELECT statement. Instead of listing all the columns in the table, we substituted an asterisk (*), which tells the RDBMS to select all columns from the table(s). We included a query in Listing 3.21 to demonstrate good coding practices. When issuing DML statements, you should verify that it was done correctly before committing the transaction. Recall from earlier discussions that DML statements require an implicit or explicit TC (transactional control) command to either ROLL BACK or COMMIT a transaction. It is a good idea to test your DML before you decide which command to issue.

DML: UPDATE COMMAND

The UPDATE command is used to modify values in the database. Line 1 in Listing 3.23 alerts the RDBMS which table is to be updated. Line 2

Listing 3.23   UPDATE Statement

```
SQL> UPDATE EMPLOYEE
  2   SET DepartmentNo = 100
  3   WHERE SSN = '123-45-6792';

1 row updated.

SQL> select *
  2   from EMPLOYEE;

SSN            FIRSTNAME   MIDDLENAME LASTNAME    DEPARTMENTNO
-------------  ----------  ---------- ----------  ------------
123-45-6789    Thomas      J.         Walker               100
123-45-6790    Terry       L.         Toye                 101
123-45-6791    Fred                   Smith                101
123-45-6792    Joseph      David      Doe                  100
```

Listing 3.24   All Rows Updated without WHERE Clause

```
SQL> UPDATE EMPLOYEE
  2   SET DepartmentNo = 100;

4 rows updated.

SQL> select *
  2   from EMPLOYEE;

SSN            FIRSTNAME   MIDDLENAME LASTNAME    DEPARTMENTNO
-------------  ----------  ---------- ----------  ------------
123-45-6789    Thomas      J.         Walker               100
123-45-6790    Terry       L.         Toye                 100
123-45-6791    Fred                   Smith                100
123-45-6792    Joseph      David      Doe                  100
```

identifies the column to be updated and the value that should be substituted. SET is a required keyword. Line 3 is extraordinarily important. Without a WHERE clause that limits the rows updated, the entire table will be updated. Listing 3.24 shows what happens when the WHERE clause is omitted. Notice that one row was updated in Listing 3.24 while four rows were updated in Listing 3.23. Again, this is one reason that DML statements should be verified before they are committed.

DML: DELETE STATEMENTS

DELETE statements are similar to UPDATE statements in that they both require WHERE clauses to limit the number of rows affected. Listing 3.25 illustrates a DELETE clause with and without a WHERE clause.

Listing 3.25   DELETE Statements

```
SQL> DELETE EMPLOYEE
  2  WHERE SSN = '123-45-6792';

1 row deleted.

SQL> SELECT *
  2  FROM EMPLOYEE;

SSN            FIRSTNAME   MIDDLENAME  LASTNAME    DEPARTMENTNO
-------------  ----------  ----------  ----------  ------------
123-45-6789    Thomas      J.          Walker               100
123-45-6790    Terry       L.          Toye                 100
123-45-6791    Fred                    Smith                100

SQL> DELETE EMPLOYEE;

3 rows deleted.

SQL> SELECT * FROM EMPLOYEE;

no rows selected
```

Line 1 uses the keyword DELETE and identifies the table to which the command will apply. Line 2 is the WHERE clause, which limits the rows affected to those we want. An important aspect of the WHERE clause is that it includes a unique condition. Notice that we used the primary key — SSN — to limit the action to one row. Notice that we always run a query to verify that the results are what we wanted before we COMMIT the transaction. Will you always know what the result will be? No, but you could say that if the number of rows deleted is greater than some anticipated count, then roll back the transaction, else commit. You can test this manually by looking at the display returned from a query, or you can use a procedural language such as PL/SQL to write the desired logic. Procedural languages are not covered in this text but several good books are on the market. Be sure you pick one that matches the procedural language recognized by your RDBMS.

TRANSACTION COMMANDS

We look at two of the transaction commands: COMMIT and ROLL BACK. If you look back at our DML commands, we have inserted a fourth row, updated a department number, and then deleted all the rows. Thus far, we have only committed the INSERT command in Listing 3.22. Therefore, we should be able to ROLL BACK all the DML commands that followed

Listing 3.26 ROLL BACK Command

```
SQL> ROLL BACK;

Rollback complete.

SQL> SELECT * FROM EMPLOYEE;

SSN             FIRSTNAME   MIDDLENAME  LASTNAME    DEPARTMENTNO
-------------   ----------  ----------  ----------  ------------
123-45-6789     Thomas      J.          Walker               100
123-45-6790     Terry       L.          Toye                 101
123-45-6791     Fred                    Smith                101
123-45-6792     Joseph      David       Doe                  102
```

the INSERT command because they have not been committed. Remember that it does not matter that we have issued more than one DML because multiple DML commands are considered a transaction and therefore transaction commands affect an entire transaction, not just a single DML. Listing 3.26 illustrates the outcome when we now issue a ROLL BACK command. Notice that we again have four rows (records). Joseph's department number remains 102, and no rows have been deleted. The syntax is simple. Line 1 shows the ROLL BACK command. The COMMIT command would be the same (see Listing 3.22).

This is an opportune time to mention that other users can query the database while DML commands are being issued. When they do, they will see the data as it was originally in the database. They will only see the changes after a COMMIT is issued. Also, while DML commands are being issued, rows in the database are locked so that others cannot attempt a change at the same time.

DCL COMMANDS

These commands are used to GRANT privileges and REVOKE privileges. A database administrator will create a user or role and then grant privileges to that user or role. Once granted, privileges can be revoked.

4

FORMAL DATA NORMALIZATION

This chapter discusses planning the structure of your database to make it easier to manage, maintain, and query. Effective structural planning helps ensure the integrity of your database and facilitates the assignment and administration of data security. Effectively structuring your database will reduce redundancies of data, thus improving disk resource usage.

Efficient database structural planning, also known as logical database design or creating the logical model, involves a process known as *normalization*. A database that has undergone the normalization process is one that has been broken down into smaller tables to reduce redundancies and aid in the management of the stored data.

Some reasons you should normalize your database to reduce data redundancy include:

- *Save disk storage space.* Historically, this was the primary reason for reducing redundancy in a database. Disk space was very expensive, and minimizing redundancy reduced disk storage requirements, which saved an expensive hardware resource. Disk cost has become much less of a determining factor over time because this resource is much less expensive today.
- *Ease of maintenance.* Updating redundant data can become a cumbersome task. If a person changes his telephone number, for example, it becomes an easy task to update the number, if it exists in only one place. When data resides in multiple locations, it can become inconsistent or out of sync if all fields are not updated simultaneously or if some occurrences of the data go unnoticed.

- *Lessen I/O activity.* Large amounts of redundant data require the manipulation of large data blocks. Because disk input/output (I/O) operations are the slowest processes within a database, reducing I/O can improve database performance significantly.
- *Query and reporting.* Un-normalized data — for example, combined fields — do not facilitate easy querying or reporting operations. When first and last names are combined into a single field, it becomes cumbersome to parse the name field by last name, as you would for a telephone directory listing.
- *Security control.* Security is easier to control when normalization has occurred because the DBA can limit table access to certain users. For example, within an employee directory, all employees may be permitted to view the name, home address, and phone number of other employees, but not their salary information.

Normalizing a database does not come without cost. Data from normalized tables must be joined to recreate the whole set of data required to satisfy a query. The joining of tables consumes both processor and I/O resources.

The normalization process involves a number of steps, each with its own set of rules. Each step of the normalization process is referred to as a "normal form." Hence, a database that satisfies the rules of the first step of normalization is said to be in the First Normal Form; one that satisfies the second normalization step is said to be in the Second Normal Form; etc. Each step within the normalization process strives to reduce data repetition or completely eliminate it.

Six levels of normalization have come into popularity in the database design world. Most developers will stop at the third level of normalization for a balance between efficiency and resource utilization. While progressing upward through the levels of normalization reduces data redundancy with a corresponding reduction in disk resource utilization, it also increases the reliance upon processor resources and increases I/O operations required to join tables of data to satisfy queries. The ultimate goal, in any normalization process, should be to achieve an effective mix between database performance and storage requirements.

Generally speaking, most databases reach an effective level of normalization, realizing a balance between storage savings and performance, at the Third Normal Form. In this discussion, we outline the steps required to reach that level and go beyond it to the Fifth Normal Form.

Now take a look at the various levels of normalization and the rules that must be satisfied to achieve each corresponding Normal Form.

DEFINITIONS OF NORMAL FORMS

Remember that there are six levels of normalization with six corresponding *normal forms*. A database's level of normalization is, therefore, referred to as its *normal form*. Conversely, the *normal form* is a way of measuring the level or depth to which a database has been normalized.

The rules of normalization are cumulative in nature, with each subsequent normal form depending upon normalization steps taken in the previous normal form. For example, a database must first be in the first normal form before it can be normalized to the second normal form, as we will see in the following definitions and examples.

The rules for normalizing tables in a database are described as follows.

First Normal Form

To begin the normalization process and achieve First Normal Form (1NF), one must:

1. Create a primary, unique key for each row of your table.
2. Eliminate any repeating groups in individual tables by moving the repeated data to newly created tables.
3. Create a primary key for each of the sets of related data that was moved to new tables.

Second Normal Form

Continuing with the intention of achieving Second Normal Form (2NF), one must adhere to the following rules:

1. Because normalization rules are cumulative, the tables must meet the rules for 1NF before they can be considered for 2NF.
2. Each column in a table must depend on the *whole* key for that table. If a column depends on only part of the key, then that column must be moved to a new table.

Third Normal Form

For a table to be in Third Normal Form (3NF), it must meet the following criteria:

1. The table must already be in the 2NF, the cumulative rule again.
2. No columns in a table can depend on any non-key column in the table.

3. You cannot have any derived data, such as total columns. Derived columns are defined in terms of other columns, rather than in terms of specific attributes.

Boyce–Codd Normal Form

This form is also known as BCNF and is often considered an extension or variation of the 3NF because it addresses situations where multiple, overlapping candidate keys exist. This can happen whenever:

1. All the candidate keys are composite keys made up of more than one column.
2. There are multiple candidate keys.
3. The candidate keys each have duplicate columns, that is, at least one column in common with another candidate key.

Fourth Normal Form

The Fourth Normal Form (4NF) applies to one-to-many and many-to-many relationships and states that independent entities cannot be stored in the same table within those relationships. You should break out any multiple sets of data that are not directly related and separate them into independent tables.

A table is therefore in Fourth Normal Form when it:

1. Is in Boyce–Codd Normal Form
2. Does not contain more than one multi-valued dependency

Fifth Normal Form

The last stage of normalization is Fifth Normal Form (5NF). This level of normalization is achieved when:

1. 4NF criteria have been met.
2. A table is in 5NF if it cannot be made into any smaller tables with different keys and the original table must be able to be reconstructed from the tables into which it has been broken down without any loss of data.
3. If you take groups of related information and horizontally segment them based on join conditions, and candidate keys within the entity accommodate each join dependency, then this type of entity is often referred to as a join-table. This form is sometimes called Projection-Join Normal Form (PJNF).

Beyond 5NF, one gets into the near-mythical territory of the Domain Key Normal Form (DKNF). If each column or domain of an entity is derived from a constraint placed on that entity to support a join, it can be referred to as DKNF. This seldom occurs in a normal world.

INTRODUCTION TO RELATIONAL ALGEBRA

E. F. Codd, an IBM researcher, is considered the father of the relational database. He developed the relational data model in 1970, by defining eight basic relational operations. In this model, all data is stored in relations, commonly known as tables. The relational algebra that these operations formulate works on relations or tables consisting of tuples or rows. The result of each of these operations can be used as the input to yet another operation; thus, we can build more elaborate expressions from these eight simplistic operations. These operations form the basics of Structured Query Languages (SQLs).

Codd's original relational algebra consisted of eight *relational operators,* separated into two groups of four operations each. The first four operations are founded upon the traditional set operations of union, intersection, difference, and Cartesian product. The last four are special operations consisting of selection (i.e., restriction), projection, join, and division. Each of these relational operators is capable of forming another table. For example, the difference between two tables has a result set consisting of another table.

Codd's original relational algebra was extended to include six *comparison operators* [=, !=, <, <=, >, and >=] and three logical operators consisting of AND, OR, and NOT. The algebra does not contain arithmetic operators or functions, making it less functional than conventional SQL.

Now take a more detailed look at each of these operators.

For two tables to be eligible for operations by union, intersection, and difference, they must have the same number of columns and their corresponding columns must be based on the same domain. The columns can, however, be named differently in each of the tables. This can be thought of as union compatibility. We will see that tables involved in a Cartesian product do not need to have union compatibility.

■ *Union.* The union of two tables ($A \cup B$) results in the set of rows of both tables combined, without any duplicates. Figure 4.1 exemplifies this operation, in which we have a table of favorite colors for different people and a table of colors that those same people wear.

■ *Intersection.* The intersection of two tables ($A \cap B$) produces the set of rows that appear in both tables, meaning they are common

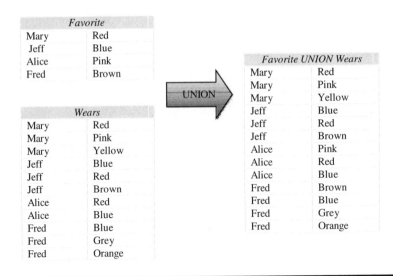

Figure 4.1 The union of two tables (Favorite UNION Wears) results in the set of rows appearing in both tables combined, without duplicates.

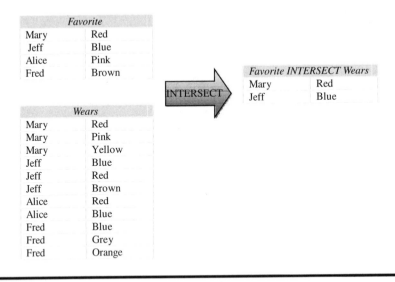

Figure 4.2 The intersection of two tables (Favorite INTERSECT Wears) results in the set of rows common to both tables.

between the tables. This is exemplified in Figure 4.2, where only two rows are common between the two example tables.

■ *Difference.* The difference between two tables (**A − B**) yields the rows from the first table in the expression that do not also exist

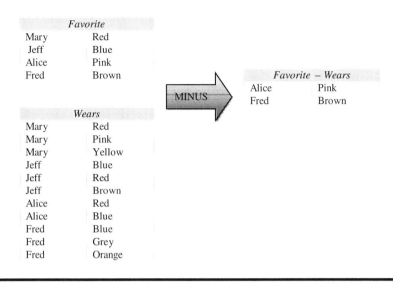

Figure 4.3 The difference between two tables (Favorite MINUS Wears) results in the set of rows from the first table that do not appear in the second table.

in the second table. This is demonstrated in Figure 4.3 where two rows (Alice–pink, Fred–brown) exist in the Favorite table, but do not appear in the Wears table.

■ *Cartesian product.* The Cartesian product of two tables (*A × B*) is an *unrestricted join* that results in each row in the first table being paired with each and every row in the second table. If there are 4 rows in the first table and 11 rows in the second table, as in our examples, then the result set will contain 44 rows (4 × 11). That is, the first row of the first table is concatenated with each and every row of the second table; then the second row of the first table is concatenated with each and every row of the second table; and so on. Figure 4.4 exemplifies this exhaustive pairing of rows.

■ *Selection.* The selection operation, also known as restriction, chooses only the rows from a table that satisfy a specified condition. The notation *T where c or* $\sigma_c(T)$ is used, where *T* is a table expression, *c* is a condition, and σ is sigma the Greek letter s (the first letter of selection). The selection operation can use any of the comparison operations (=, !=, <=, <, >=, >) explained later in this chapter. Selection operations are identified by the use of the WHERE clause in an expression. In Figure 4.5, two rows satisfy the "WHERE name = 'Alice'" clause. The WHERE clause can also contain any of three logical operators defined as AND, OR, and NOT. We can see an example of the logical operator OR included in the expression exemplified by Figure 4.6.

Favorite × Wears			
Favorite.Name	Favorite.Color	Wears.Name	Wears.Color
Mary	Red	Mary	Red
Mary	Red	Mary	Pink
Mary	Red	Mary	Yellow
Mary	Red	Jeff	Blue
Mary	Red	Jeff	Red
Mary	Red	Jeff	Brown
Mary	Red	Alice	Red
Mary	Red	Alice	Blue
Mary	Red	Fred	Blue
Mary	Red	Fred	Grey
Mary	Red	Fred	Orange
Jeff	Blue	Mary	Red
Jeff	Blue	Mary	Pink
Jeff	Blue	Mary	Yellow
Jeff	Blue	Jeff	Blue
Jeff	Blue	Jeff	Red
Jeff	Blue	Jeff	Brown
Jeff	Blue	Alice	Red
Jeff	Blue	Alice	Blue
Jeff	Blue	Fred	Blue
Jeff	Blue	Fred	Grey
Jeff	Blue	Fred	Orange
Alice	Pink	Mary	Red
Alice	Pink	Mary	Pink
Alice	Pink	Mary	Yellow
Alice	Pink	Jeff	Blue
Alice	Pink	Jeff	Red
Alice	Pink	Jeff	Brown
Alice	Pink	Alice	Red
Alice	Pink	Alice	Blue
Alice	Pink	Fred	Blue
Alice	Pink	Fred	Grey
Alice	Pink	Fred	Orange
Fred	Brown	Mary	Red
Fred	Brown	Mary	Pink
Fred	Brown	Mary	Yellow
Fred	Brown	Jeff	Blue
Fred	Brown	Jeff	Red
Fred	Brown	Jeff	Brown
Fred	Brown	Alice	Red
Fred	Brown	Alice	Blue
Fred	Brown	Fred	Blue
Fred	Brown	Fred	Grey
Fred	Brown	Fred	Orange

Favorite	
Name	Color
Mary	Red
Jeff	Blue
Alice	Pink
Fred	Brown

TIMES

Wears	
Name	Color
Mary	Red
Mary	Pink
Mary	Yellow
Jeff	Blue
Jeff	Red
Jeff	Brown
Alice	Red
Alice	Blue
Fred	Blue
Fred	Grey
Fred	Orange

Figure 4.4   The Cartesian product of two tables (Favorite TIMES Wears) results in each row in the first table being paired with each and every row in the second table.

Wears	
Name	*Color*
Mary	Red
Mary	Pink
Mary	Yellow
Jeff	Blue
Jeff	Red
Jeff	Brown
Alice	Red
Alice	Blue
Fred	Blue
Fred	Grey
Fred	Orange

WHERE ⟹

WHERE name = 'Alice'	
Name	*Color*
Alice	Red
Alice	Blue

Figure 4.5 **The selection expression results in a subset of rows which satisfy the condition expressed by the WHERE clause (i.e., when the WHERE condition evaluates to TRUE).**

Wears	
Name	*Color*
Mary	Red
Mary	Pink
Mary	Yellow
Jeff	Blue
Jeff	Red
Jeff	Brown
Alice	Red
Alice	Blue
Fred	Blue
Fred	Grey
Fred	Orange

WHERE ⟹

WHERE name = 'Alice' OR color = 'Grey'	
Name	*Color*
Alice	Red
Alice	Blue
Fred	Grey

Figure 4.6 **Here, the selection expression includes the logical operator OR. In this case, the resulting set of rows satisfies either the "name = 'Alice'" OR the "color = 'Grey'" expression.**

- *Projection.* The projection operation can be defined as the selection of one or more columns from a table, while eliminating any duplicate rows from the resulting set. This produces a column subset, also called a vertical subset. We can represent the projection operation by *T[c1, c2, ...]*, where *T* is a table expression and *[c1, c2, ...]* is a column list, also called a projection list. Figure 4.7 shows an example of projection.
- *Join.* Now take a look at relational join operations between two tables. A relational join compares column attributes within the

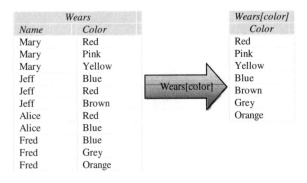

Wears	
Name	*Color*
Mary	Red
Mary	Pink
Mary	Yellow
Jeff	Blue
Jeff	Red
Jeff	Brown
Alice	Red
Alice	Blue
Fred	Blue
Fred	Grey
Fred	Orange

Wears[color]
Color
Red
Pink
Yellow
Blue
Brown
Grey
Orange

Figure 4.7   The projection *wears[color]* selects unique values from the table (wears) and column(s) listed (color).

tables using the comparison operators (=. !=, <, <=, >, >=). Columns being compared must have the same definition but they can be named differently. If the column names are the same in each table, then fully qualified names are used in the form *table-name.column-name*. The join of table A with table B using column attributes a and b, respectively, yields the Cartesian product of $A \times B$, restricted by the comparison of the column attributes. If the comparison operator is =, then the restriction is where $A.a = B.b$, which can also be indicated as '$A \times B$ *where c*', c being the comparison or join condition. When the comparison operator is =, the join is known as an equi-join. Compound join conditions, such as $A.a = B.b$ *and* $A.x < B.x$, are allowed as indicated by:

$$A \times B \text{ where } A.a = B.b \text{ and } A.x < B.x$$

Because the resulting table is a Cartesian product, it contains the total number of columns in A and B. Due to the restriction process, the resulting table normally has fewer rows than the product of the number of rows in each table, as in a true Cartesian product. Figure 4.8 exemplifies a compound join condition.

■ *Division*. The final operation is relational division. A table is only divisible by another table when the first table A consists of more columns than the second table B. If there are n columns in table B, then we can define the results of the operation $A \div B$ when the last n columns of A are paired with all of the rows of B in order; then the result is the remaining columns of the paired rows of table A minus any duplicates. This can be demonstrated best through an example, as shown in Figure 4.9.

Favorite Name	Color
Mary	Red
Jeff	Blue
Alice	Pink
Fred	Brown

Favorite × Wears where Favorite.Name = Wears.Name and Favorite.Color <> Wears.Color

Favorite.Name	Favorite.Color	Wears.Name	Wears.Color
Mary	Red	Mary	Pink
Mary	Red	Mary	Yellow
Jeff	Blue	Jeff	Red
Jeff	Blue	Jeff	Brown
Alice	Pink	Alice	Red
Alice	Pink	Alice	Blue
Fred	Brown	Fred	Blue
Fred	Brown	Fred	Grey
Fred	Brown	Fred	Orange

JOIN where

Wears Name	Color
Mary	Red
Mary	Pink
Mary	Yellow
Jeff	Blue
Jeff	Red
Jeff	Brown
Alice	Red
Alice	Blue
Fred	Blue
Fred	Grey
Fred	Orange

Figure 4.8 The join of two tables (Favorite × Wears where Favorite.Name = Wears.Name and Favorite.Color <> Wears.Color) results in the restricted Cartesian product as shown.

COMPARISON OPERATIONS AND LOGICAL OPERATORS

We have mentioned comparison operators, logical operators, and relational operators in previous discussions, but how are they evaluated when used together in compound expressions?

Recall that the comparison operators are defined as follows:

= Equals
!= Not equal
<= Less than or equal (subset)
< Less than (proper subset)
>= Greater than or equal (superset)
> Greater than (proper superset)

These comparison operators have top priority and are always evaluated first in a compound expression. Because they have equal priority, the comparison operators are evaluated from left to right in an expression.

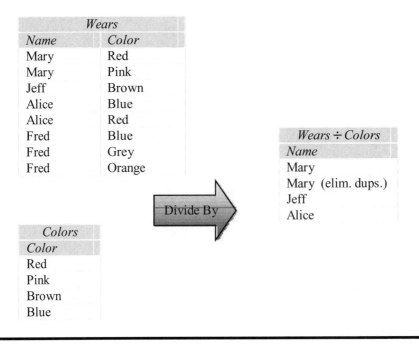

Figure 4.9 The division *Wears ÷ Colors* yields results when the last columns of the Wears table are matched by all columns in the Colors table in order of appearance. Duplicates are eliminated.

The logical operators NOT, AND, and OR are evaluated in priority sequence as listed. That is, NOT has first priority, AND has second priority, and OR has third priority among the logical operators.

Last on the priority list are the remaining six relational operators of union, intersection, difference, Cartesian product, natural join, and division. These six operators are evaluated from left to right with equal priority.

It must be noted that you can control the sequence of expression evaluation by using parentheses. Expressions enclosed in parentheses are evaluated first, starting with the inner-most parentheses set and working outward. Expressions within parentheses at the same level are evaluated left to right.

Figure 4.10 is a prioritized listing of the comparison, logical, and relational operators.

Now let us take a practical example and apply the rules of normalization to exemplify how database normalization works.

APPLYING NORMAL FORMS

Once you have your list of data items, you are ready to start normalizing your data. As you begin, it is a good idea to limit your efforts to developing

Priority	Type	Operator
1	Comparison	= <> < <= > >=
2		NOT
3	Logical	AND
4		OR
5		Selection Projection
6	Relational	Union (∪), Intersection (∩), Difference (−), Cartesian product (×), *natural join* (*A*×*B* *where*), and *division* (÷)

Figure 4.10   The prioritized order of evaluation for *Comparison, Logical,* and *Relational* operators.

a data diagram using pencil and paper. You should never attempt to create and normalize your tables without first working through the entire process on paper; developing a data diagram will save you both time and the potential for error. As with any development project, a good *rule of thumb* is: The more time spent planning, the less time spent implementing and debugging.

XYZ Company has two secure parking garages — an east garage and a west garage. Employees have transponders (radio devices) attached to the windshield of their vehicles that open the garage door as they approach it. Some employees have multiple vehicles and have requested that they be issued a transponder for each vehicle. The administration department must keep track of the transponders issued to each employee and retrieve the transponders from the employee upon termination.

The first step will be to identify the entities with which we are working. Entities are a group of one type of data. Our example database will store data related to two entities: Employees and Transponders. The number of entities may increase as we begin to normalize the data.

Figure 4.11 shows the Employees table as it was initially constructed from the data collected on forms submitted by the Administration department.

Notice that there are two columns within the table that are allocated for recording transponder numbers. This was done to accommodate employees with multiple vehicles; but what happens when an employee has more than two vehicles? You may also notice that the employee's entire name is contained in a single column. This is not very conducive to listing the employees in alphabetical order by last name, in a directory format.

Employee Name	Department	Transponder 1	Transponder 2
Amber Schneider	Finance	E – 0010	E – 0011
Clarence Moore	Engineering	W – 0020	
Dorothy Claiborne	Development	W – 0022	
Jennifer Stephens	Administration	E – 0005	
Mary Jones	Sales	E – 0007	E – 0009
Nancy Stephens	Finance	E – 0006	
Rudy Dumas	Development	W – 0005	W – 0006
William Peters	Information Technology	W – 0001	

Figure 4.11 Employees table lists employees with transponders as data was collected (un-normalized).

First Normal Form

You may recall, from our earlier definition, that 1NF involves the elimination of repeating groups of data as is recognized in our example by the repetition of transponder numbers and about assuring the atomicity of data-independent and self-contained — contrary to the name field in our example. It also involves the creation of a primary key and moving repetitive data to new tables, while creating new keys for the new tables. Thus, from our original definition, to create a First Normal Form complicate table, we must:

1. Create a primary, unique key for each row of our table.
2. Eliminate any repeating groups in individual tables by moving the repeated data to newly created tables.
3. Create a primary key for each of the sets of related data that was moved to new tables.

Second Normal Form

You will recall that to achieve Second Normal Form, you move data that only partly depends on the primary key into another table. Each new table created refers to its parent via a foreign key. The rules were previously stated as follows:

1. Because normalization rules are cumulative, the tables must meet the rules for 1NF before they can be considered for 2NF.
2. Each column in a table must depend on the *whole* key for that table. If a column depends on only part of the key, then that column must be moved to a new table.

Figures 4.12, 4.13, and 4.14 show our resulting tables after applying 2NF rules.

Employee ID	First Name	Last Name	Department	Transponder
1	Amber	Schneider	Finance	E0010
1	Amber	Schneider	Finance	E0011
2	Clarence	Moore	Engineering	W0020
3	Dorothy	Claiborne	Development	W0022
4	Jennifer	Stephens	Administration	E0005
5	Mary	Jones	Sales	E0007
5	Mary	Jones	Sales	E0009
6	Nancy	Stephens	Finance	E0006
7	Rudy	Dumas	Development	W0005
7	Rudy	Dumas	Development	W0006
8	William	Peters	I.T.	W0001

Figure 4.12 Employee table after applying 1NF rules.

Employees Table

Employee ID	First Name	Last Name	Department
1	Amber	Schneider	Finance
2	Clarence	Moore	Engineering
3	Dorothy	Claiborne	Development
4	Jennifer	Stephens	Administration
5	Mary	Jones	Sales
6	Nancy	Stephens	Finance
7	Rudy	Dumas	Development
8	William	Peters	I.T.

Transponders Table

TID (PK)	Employee ID(FK)	Transponder
1	1	E0010
2	1	E0011
3	2	W0020
4	3	W0022
5	4	E0005
6	5	E0007
7	5	E0009
8	6	E0006
9	7	W0005
10	7	W0006
11	8	W0001

Figure 4.13 Employees with transponders after applying 2NF rules.

When the primary key is based on more than one field (i.e., a composite key), all non-key values must depend on the entire compound primary key, not just on one value or field within the key. Any non-key value that does not support the primary key should be moved to another table.

Employee Table

Employee ID	First Name	Last Name
1	Amber	Schneider
2	Clarence	Moore
3	Dorothy	Claiborne
4	Jennifer	Stephens
5	Mary	Jones
6	Nancy	Stephens
7	Rudy	Dumas
8	William	Peters

Transponder Table

TID (PK)	Employee ID(FK)	Transponder
1	1	E0010
2	1	E0011
3	2	W0020
4	3	W0022
5	4	E0005
6	5	E0007
7	5	E0009
8	6	E0006
9	7	W0005
10	7	W0006
11	8	W0001

Employee Department Table

Employee ID (PK)	Department ID(FK)
1	1
2	2
3	3
4	4
5	5
6	1
7	3
8	6

Department Table

Department ID (PK)	Department
1	Finance
2	Engineering
3	Development
4	Administration
5	Sales
6	I.T.

Figure 4.14 Employees with transponders after applying 3NF rules.

Third Normal Form

The Third Normal Form rules essentially state that any value that describes a non-key field must be moved to another table. That is, you must remove any data in a table that does not depend on the primary key.

The three rules of 3NF are:

1. The table must already be in the 2NF, the cumulative rule again.
2. No columns in a table can depend upon any non-key column in the table.
3. You cannot have any derived data, such as total columns. Derived columns are defined in terms of other columns, rather than in terms of specific attributes.

Boyce–Codd Normal Form

This is the point where many developers begin to disagree on the effective level of normalization for efficient database design. Many stop at 3NF, claiming loss of performance when achieving BCNF and beyond.

For this level, there must be no non-key-dependent fields. This sub-rule of 3NF catches whatever values might fall through the cracks in the 3NF rules. Any field that shows a dependence on any non-key value must be moved to another table.

Fourth Normal Form

The 4NF requires that independent entities cannot be stored in the same table in a many-to-many relationship. To achieve 4NF, you should break up tables into new ones to store the independent entities.

Fifth Normal Form

The 5NF guards against data loss by insisting that you be able to reconstruct the original table from the tables into which it has been broken down. The 5NF rule ensures that you do not create extra columns in tables, and that all the table structures are only as inclusive as absolutely required.

SUMMARY

Normalizing your database provides a number of benefits, some of which include:

- *Save disk storage space.* Disk cost has become much less of a determining factor over time because this resource is much less expensive today.
- *Ease of maintenance.* When data resides in multiple locations, the data can become inconsistent or out of sync if all fields are not updated simultaneously or if some occurrences of the data go unnoticed.

- *Lessen I/O activity.* Because disk I/O operations are the slowest processes within a database, reducing I/O can improve database performance significantly.
- *Query and reporting.* Un-normalized data — for example, combined fields — do not facilitate easy querying or reporting operations.
- *Security control.* Security is easier to control when normalization has occurred because the DBA can limit table access to certain users.

Normalizing a database does not come without cost. Data from normalized tables must be joined to recreate the whole set of data required to satisfy a query. The joining of tables consumes both processor and I/O resources. Your ultimate goal in any normalization process should be to achieve an effective mix between database performance and storage requirements.

No one knows your data better than you do, and each circumstance is unique. Your situation may require a combination of normalized and denormalized data to provide the best solution. Always normalize your data first, and denormalize the data only on a case-by-case basis to solve unique situations. If you start by establishing denormalized data, you will ultimately fail in producing a solid data model.

Chapter 5 discusses when and why you might want to denormalize data.

5

DATA
DENORMALIZATION

This chapter discusses database denormalization. The denormalization process may involve recombining separate normalized tables or creating duplicate data within tables to eliminate table joins when satisfying queries. Some may think of this as just the opposite of what we spent the entire previous chapter doing. So why did we normalize the database in the first place? Well, the answer to that question is that we should always normalize our database first to reap the benefits of a normalized model, primarily, that of data integrity. You should never start out with the thought in mind that you will denormalize your data. Denormalization should only be done on a case-by-case basis, for example, when the performance of a particular query is unacceptable due to the large number of table joins that must occur to satisfy the query.

HISTORICAL PERSPECTIVE ON DISK COSTS

You will recall that one of the historical reasons for normalizing a database was to reduce data redundancy to save costly disk resources. That was back in the days when a disk drive was housed in a cabinet the size of a washing machine and it would take a room full of those drives to begin to approach the storage capacity of a modest laptop computer today.

In 1970, an IBM model 3330-1 disk had a capacity of 100 MB and cost $25,970, for a cost per megabyte of $259.70. By the year 2000, you could buy a Seagate Elite 47 GB SCSI drive for $695 at a cost per megabyte of less than 1.5 cents. Using this example, over the course of 30 years, the cost of disk resources became 17,000 times less expensive.

Figure 5.1 shows pictures of two models of those old disk technologies.

IBM model 1311 disk – 2MB (1964)   DEC RP06 disk – 178MB

Figure 5.1 Washing machine size disk drives. Left: IBM model 1311 disk (2 MB); and Right: DEC RP06 disk (178 MB).

Because disks are dramatically less expensive today, reducing data redundancy to save disk space is no longer a reason to normalize a database.

THE IMPORTANCE OF DATABASE PERFORMANCE TO THE LOGICAL MODEL

Database performance should always be your primary concern. You may recall from the previous chapter that as you move up the normalization scale with your database design, you may recognize slowed response times. That is, as the normalization level increases, performance sometimes decreases. Remember that as you implement the normalization rules, you create more and more tables. These tables must then be joined to solve queries, and the joining process consumes both CPU and I/O resources.

What a dilemma, you say. Why then did we bother with normalizing the database? You will recall that normalization also aids in the maintenance of data integrity within the database. If you need to change a data entity, it is easiest to do if that entity occurs in only one place. Eliminating redundancy ensures that there is only one occurrence of the data and eliminates any worries about overlooking an occurrence or about having multiple occurrences get out of sync.

The reasoning behind denormalization, then, is to strike a balance between storage optimization and database performance.

INTRODUCING DATA REDUNDANCY: SIZE VERSUS VOLATILITY

Because performance is our primary concern, and we confirm that denormalizing our database improves performance, we must weigh the performance improvement against the potential for maintenance nightmares and consequential data integrity issues.

Here are a few things to consider when trying to decide whether to denormalize your data model:

- Sometimes you can eliminate a considerable number of table joins that are required to satisfy a query just by adding a single denormalized column to a table, significantly improving the query performance. For example, adding a *year_to_date_dollars* summation column to the *customer* table could eliminate joins to the *order* table and to the *order_detail* table to sum the information. Since orders can be a volatile area to deal with, you must remember to update the *year_to_date_dollars* column whenever new orders are entered or when the year changes. This could be done through the use of a trigger on the *order_detail* table and through a process included within year-end processing to reset the summations. Also, because of the volatility factor, you must weigh any performance loss you may realize during INSERT, UPDATE, and DELETE operations performed on the *order_detail* table due to the need to also update the *customer* table. Generally speaking, you are better off concentrating denormalization on nonvolatile fields (those that are updated infrequently).

- If the data is fairly static (is seldom updated), getting data out of sync after denormalizing becomes less of an issue, as does any worry about affecting the performance of INSERT, UPDATE, and DELETE operations. If, for example, your design is for a data warehouse database, used solely for reporting, you would have very little concern about volatile data changes potentially causing redundant data to get out of sync. We discuss special data warehouse situations a little later in this chapter.

- When it comes to reporting, sophisticated end users have more refined and powerful reporting tools and have become more savvy at creating their own reports. Simplifying the data model through denormalization could not only improve their query performance, but the denormalized structure also provides the end user with a more simplistic, easier-to-understand look at the database.

There are several theories and methods that can be applied when you begin to approach the topic of denormalization. Let us take a look at some of these.

THE THEORY OF DR. RALPH KIMBALL

When we have huge volumes of data used mostly for querying, such as in a data warehouse application, again performance is of the utmost importance. With data warehouses, we have no concern about data integrity issues because the data is read-only. There is no need to worry about replicated entities getting out of sync or about the performance of INSERT, UPDATE, and DELETE statements because we are not performing these operations. The data warehouse is an ideal situation in which to implement denormalization.

Dr. Ralph Kimball developed a new model specifically for the denormalization of data warehouse databases. Kimball's architecture consists of a dimensional approach to modeling versus what we have been discussing thus far, which is known as entity-relationship modeling. In contrast to the entity-relationship model, which describes entities and relationships between entities stored in the database, the Kimball model describes data in terms of dimensions and facts. Those dimensions and facts become tables within the database.

A simple dimensional model consists of a fact table, which is typically the largest table within the database, and many smaller dimension tables. The fact table is where all of the detail information is stored and the dimension tables are where the static reference information is stored. For example, the fact table might contain all of the detailed order information, while one dimension table might contain customer information (cust_name, cust_address, etc.) and another dimension table might contain product information (product_name, product_description, etc.). Whereas the entity-relationship model is very complex in structure, the dimensional model is very simplistic, as demonstrated by Figure 5.2. Structural simplicity is what provides performance to the dimensional model.

Kimball's dimensional model has become known as the *Star Join* data construct because of its appearance, as indicated in Figure 5.2.

PRE-JOINING ENTITIES TOGETHER

Some database engines, such as Oracle, allow you to pre-join entities together using specialized views. If you are using an Oracle database, this concept is referred to as creating *Materialized Views*. This concept has also been referred to as a *snapshot*.

The database supplies the architect with packages to be invoked to create the materialized view snapshots and for refreshing those snapshots as the pre-joined information becomes stale. The snapshot is used to create a flattened view of the required data without actually denormalizing the underlying table structure. This is demonstrated in Figure 5.3.

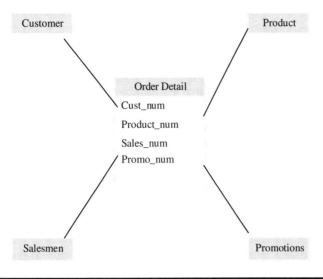

Figure 5.2   Dimensional modeling ... star join.

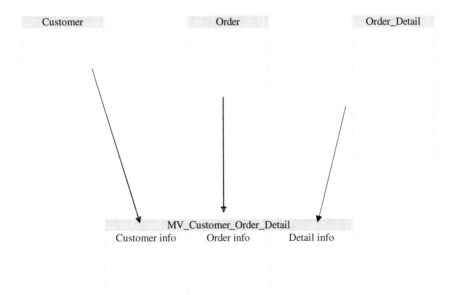

Figure 5.3   Pre-joining data.

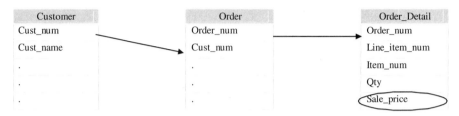

Table joins required to sum year-to-date dollars information

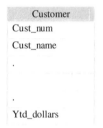

Joins eliminated via the creation of asummation field in the customer table

---

Figure 5.4   Creating pre-aggregated summary information.

PRE-AGGREGATING SUMMARY INFORMATION

As mentioned in an earlier example, creating summary information can reduce the need to perform multiple table joins to satisfy query results. Of course, including summary information in our records violates our goal of the 3NF level of normalization, but then that is what denormalization is really all about. The summation field also presents a synchronization challenge. Whenever *order_detail* information changes due to new orders, order cancellations, etc., the summation field in the *customer* table record must be updated or that information will become stale. One of the best ways to keep this field in sync is to create a trigger on the *order_detail* table that fires when records are inserted, updated, or deleted. The additional processing time imposed by the update of the summation field during Data Manipulation Language (DML) operations on the *order_detail* table would need to be weighed against the performance improvement realized by the elimination of table joins to satisfy queries.

Figure 5.4 exemplifies our discussion of creating a *year_to_date_dollars* summation column in the *customer* table to avoid joins with the *order* table and with the *order_detail* table to speed up queries for year-to-date information, especially when that is a frequently occurring query.

NON-FIRST NORMAL FORM ENTITIES

Of course, one of the easiest ways to denormalize is to simply undo what was done during the normalization process. Reiterating, we would only do this in an effort to improve the performance of a frequently executed query without causing ourselves too much consternation regarding data integrity issues or volume of data issues caused by redundancy.

Some of the obvious things that we could do would be to restore duplicate keys and restore duplicate attributes.

HORIZONTAL AND VERTICAL PARTITIONING FOR PERFORMANCE

Some would argue that partitioning does not violate normalization rules, but they should be reminded that the rules of normalization insist that only one table should exist per entity in a database. Partitioning is accomplished by splitting tables either by rows (horizontal partitioning) or by columns (vertical partitioning). Why would we consider doing this to improve performance?

Over time, tables can become quite large and performance degrades as larger and larger amounts of data are scanned to satisfy a query. One way to improve performance, then, would be to reduce the table size. If a large table contains data that can be arranged by a date or some other value, we should be able to partition the table horizontally into one or more smaller tables.

As an example, take a look at the *orders* table used earlier. Because orders are entered by date and because there comes a time after orders are shipped that the order becomes eligible for archiving, we could effectively partition the *orders* table horizontally by *order_date* or maybe *ship_date*. For example, orders that were shipped more than 60 or 90 days ago are probably not referenced very often and could be moved to another partition, thus reducing the size of the 'active orders' partition. Data from all partitions would still be available (via union) for quarterly and annual summations, but the 'active orders' partition would be more compact and faster to scan (see Figure 5.5).

OK, that makes sense, but where does vertical partitioning come into play? Well, we know that tables reside on disk and that they must be read into memory buffers to be processed. Those memory buffers have a finite size that we have to work with. Once tables are read into the memory buffer, scanning and processing the information is very fast. It stands to reason, then, that the more of a table that we can fit into memory, the faster the performance we will realize. One way to get more of a table into memory is to partition it vertically.

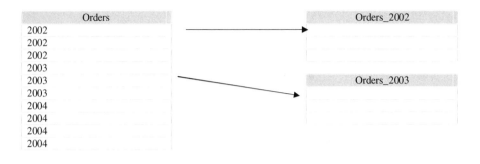

Figure 5.5 Horizontal partitioning.

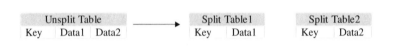

Figure 5.6 Vertical partitioning.

For example, assume that we have a large table with many wide rows. Also assume that a set of fields in the row is referenced very infrequently. We might then consider splitting the less referenced fields into a new table, reducing the size of our original table. With a reduced row width, we can then fit more of our frequently referenced table into the memory buffer where response time is very fast (see Figure 5.6).

SUMMARY

In this chapter we learned that denormalization is not only acceptable, but it is sometimes a necessity to provide acceptable database performance. You should always start by normalizing your database to establish a benchmark. If, after normalization, database response is acceptable, then there is no reason to even consider denormalization. If response is unacceptable, however, then you should attempt to increase performance through denormalization on a case-by-case basis.

Some approaches to denormalization include:

- Adding redundant columns
- Adding derived columns
- Partitioning tables (horizontally or vertically)
- Use dimensional modeling (star join)

Data warehouse databases have very different requirements from those of OLTP-type applications. The data warehouse can be freely denormalized without the fear of losing data integrity, because the data is, by and large, read-only. There is little concern with affecting DML activity on the data warehouse, because it does not exist.

Data warehouses can take advantage of dimensional modeling (the star join) conceptualized by Dr. Ralph Kimball. With the star join, you normally have one or two very large tables containing detail information called the fact table(s) and many smaller tables with static reference tables called dimension tables. It is not uncommon for the fact table to be very wide and to contain millions of records.

6

OBJECT-ORIENTED DESIGN

Object-oriented programming has been around for a number of years and is experiencing wide use. In the early 1990s, the database community believed that as programs became object-oriented, the database management system would also need to change. The database's job is to provide persistence to the data used in the object-oriented program. Because the program is designed to manipulate an object, the database should only need to store and retrieve the object. Of course, the reality is more difficult to implement. Although there are a number of pure object-oriented database management systems, most enterprise-level programs use an object-relational approach that combines some of the capability of object-oriented programs with the proven ability of enterprise-level relational database management systems. Chapter 7 discusses the object-relational design approach.

Object-oriented systems development is a natural extension of the structured programming approach. Just as structured programming emphasized the benefits of properly nested loop structures, object-oriented development emphasizes the benefits of modular and reusable computer code, and the benefits of modeling real-world objects. Traditionally, programs were designed by focusing on what the program was meant to do. This focus was on the functional or structural requirements. In object-oriented programming, the focus is on the data, or object.

In general, an object is a set of related data along with a set of methods to act on that data. An object has a state defined by the values of the data that makes up the object. To change the state, the program would call one of the object's methods. In Table 6.1, the object has a state of

Table 6.1   Example Object

Variable:	
CurrentState = TRUE;	
Methods:	
setFalse	CurrentState = FALSE;
setTrue	CurrentState = TRUE;
changeState	if (CurrentState = TRUE)
	then CurrentState = FALSE
	else CurrentState = TRUE;
getState	return CurrentState;

true or false. To change the object's state, one can call one of the methods the object provides.

The object is created with CurrentState = TRUE. One can find out what the state of the object is by calling the object's method called getState, which will return the value of the CurrentState variable. One can change the state by calling the changeState method or set the state as desired by calling the setFalse or setTrue methods. The object has a public interface, which is defined as those methods that can be called from the outside to the object. Other "private" methods can only be called by methods internal to the object. This is called encapsulation and is used to protect the object from having the program improperly change its state.

Most object-oriented programs refer to an object definition as a class. The class defines the data and methods that make up an object of that class. For example, one can have a class called Employee, and then create two objects of the Employee class, one called TOM and the other called SAM (Table 6.2). Once created, one can call the public methods to retrieve or change the object's state. To give TOM a raise, one calls the giveRaise method.

```
Tom.giveRaise(1.1);
```

Now the TOM object will have a 10 percent increase in salary.

Every object that the program creates will have the same variables and methods that are defined within the class Employee.

Inheritance is another characteristic of object-oriented programs. Inheritance allows the programmer to define a class and then create subclasses that inherit the main class's attributes. The classic example is to define a class called motor. A class can then be defined called vehicle that inherits the class motor. Now each vehicle object will also contain all the attributes contained in the class motor. Those attributes are inherited from the motor class.

Table 6.2   Employee Objects

Variable:		
first_name; last_name; emp_no; salary;		

Methods:

```
GetName          return (first_name, last_name);
getEmpData       return(emp_no, salary);
giveRaise(num)   salary = salary*num;
```

TOM		SAM
First_name = Tom; Last_name = Winkler; Emp_no = 1001; Salary = 10,000;		First_name = Sam; Last_name = Thumb; Emp_no = 1003; Salary = 10,000;

Once the data is designed into objects with the required methods to manipulate their states, the program consists of the code necessary to tie the object behavior together. There are many advantages to designing programs using object-oriented design. One is that the program is inherently modular. Extending and maintaining code is easier because all the variables and the methods that act on them are in one modular object. This is, of course, an over-simplification of object-oriented programming. The reality is that object-oriented programming has a steep learning curve and can be quite difficult for a structure-trained programmer to implement.

With programs moving quickly to object-oriented designs, the next logical step in database design is the object-oriented technology method. Object-oriented databases will not only store data and the relationships between data, but also the behavior of the data. Once data behaviors are added to a database management system, these "intelligent" databases will dramatically change the development of database systems.

OBJECT-ORIENTED TERMINOLOGY

Classes

- A class is a template for a group of objects.
- A class is a definition with common variables and methods.
- Classes are hierarchical in nature.
- Classes can have subclasses.
- Classes are sometimes referred to as an object type.

Objects

- An object is an instance of a class.
- Each object is given a unique object identifier when it is created.
- When an object is created, it "inherits" all data attributes from the class definition.
- When a method is requested against an object, it inherits all methods from its class and its superclasses.
- Each object has its own private data storage area in memory.
- Each object has public interfaces.

Messages

Messages are the calls to an object's public methods. There is not a physical message; rather, it is the method call, passing the necessary parameters. Below are some examples of messages:

```
order_total = compute_order_total(123);
                    /* This returns an integer */
credit_status = check_customer_credit("jones");
                    /* This returns a Boolean */
Update_inventory_level("widget", 37373);
                    /* This does not return a value */
```

The message with the parameters being sent must match one of the object's public methods in order to perform the requested operation. If the message does not call an object's public method or the parameters are not the correct type, an error will occur.

Abstract Classes

An abstract class is a class that is never instantiated. That is, an abstract class serves only to pass data structures and methods to lower-level classes. An abstract class is a class that has no objects; it is put in the class hierarchy mainly to just help organize the structure. Subclasses of the abstract class can have objects.

Encapsulation

Encapsulation gathers the data and methods of an object and puts them into a package, creating a well-defined boundary around the object. Encapsulation is often referred to as information hiding, and can be used to restrict which users and what operations can be performed against the data inside the object.

Classes provide encapsulation or information hiding by access control. A class will grant or deny access to its objects using the *public* and *private* access specifics. Public members define an interface between a class and the users of that class. Public members can be accessed by any function in a program. Objects can contain both public and private variables; the *public* variables are used with the object's methods or interfaces.

Private variables are only known to the object and cannot be accessed by an interface. For example, a private method might be used to compute an internal value.

Inheritance

Two of the benefits of object technology (OT) are code reusability and extensibility, and inheritance allows the implementation of both these features. When new objects are created, they can inherit the data attributes or variables from their class and all classes above them in the class hierarchy. Because a method is procedural code, when an object inherits methods, it is inheriting the programming code associated with the method.

Inheritance is an easy concept to understand, and also a very powerful concept when a class is broken down into another class or classes. The class that was broken down is called the superclass and the resulting class or classes are called subclasses. These subclasses then inherit all the methods and variables that the superclass has. By using inheritance we do not have to repeat the methods or variables in each of the subclasses and therefore do not have to produce any programming code in the subclass for the inherited methods.

One class can inherit attributes from multiple other classes. For example, the Vehicle class inherits from the Motor class. It could also inherit from other classes such as the Drive_train class, the Lighting class, and the Steering class. All of these classes contain attributes that help define objects in the Vehicle class.

Polymorphism

Polymorphism is the ability of different objects to receive the same message and respond in different ways. Polymorphism simplifies the communication between objects using a common interface to hide different implementation details. Polymorphism adds a high degree of flexibility to OT by allowing the addition of new objects to a computer system without modifying existing procedures, helping to reduce maintenance and allowing systems to change more rapidly as customer needs change.

In the example discussed previously, a class Motor was defined and a subclass Vehicle inherited the Motor class. If one creates three objects from class Vehicle, they will each inherit the Motor attributes. If there are three Vehicle objects (Car, Boat, Airplane), then there are three Vehicle objects that can have significantly different motors. The Car object has an air-cooled, eight-cylinder, gas-fueled motor, while the Boat object has a water-cooled, six-cylinder, gas-fueled motor. The Airplane object might have a jet engine. The Motor class defined a public method called start_engine that is used to change the state of a variable to running. How that method functions on objects Car and Boat may be the same; however, on object Airplane, the start_engine method is entirely different. The Airplane object will "overload" the start_engine method so that it properly functions on a jet engine. Overloading is basically the ability of a programming method to perform more than one kind of operation, depending on the context in which the method is used.

Containment

Containment is the ability of an object to be made up of other objects. This is similar to inheritance except that instead of inheriting the attributes of a superclass, the object has an attribute that is the superclass. For example, a Vehicle object called Car might inherit the attributes of the Motor class and it might contain an object called brakes that is a Brake class. The advantages of inheritance and containment are in modularizing the Vehicle object. A programmer can improve the Brake class and the improvement will apply to the Vehicle object.

Extensibility

Extensibility is an especially powerful concept that allows an object-oriented database to handle novel data situations easily. Extensibility is the ability of an object-oriented system to add new behaviors to an existing system without changing the entire application.

Let us assume that we want to create a new object, Future_vehicle. The new class only needs to define attributes not already defined in the Vehicle class and overload those methods that require different behavior. Once defined, Future_vehicle objects can be created within the existing program.

Object Identity

Object identity is an important concept when talking about an object-oriented database. Every object must have some method to identify it (not necessarily uniquely). When an object is created in a program, it uses some type of name, which is a pointer to the object in memory. In an earlier example, we created an object TOM from the Employee class:

Table 6.3   Information in a Relational Database

EMP_NO	FIRST NAME	LAST NAME	DEPT
1001	TOM	WINKLER	FINANCE
1005	SAM	SPADE	SECURITY
1008	TOM	JONES	PERSONNEL

```
employee TOM = new employee;
```

Access to this object is through the reference TOM:

```
TOM.giveRaise(1.1);
```

The above code gave TOM a 10 percent raise or, more accurately, the salary attribute of the TOM object was increased by 10 percent. Once the program ends, the TOM object is lost. If I need to keep the TOM object, it must be stored in some type of persistent store, in this case a database. Because the identity of the TOM object is the reference in memory, we need some way to identify the TOM object in the database. Otherwise, we will not be able to find the TOM object from the other Employee objects in the database.

In a relational database, information is identified by values such as primary keys. In an Employee table, an employee can be identified by the employee number, such as in Table 6.3. The employee number uniquely identifies the employee and is the primary key for the table. A search for employees with the first name of TOM could return many employees and the program would have to process them all or use some other criteria to locate the specific TOM employee needed.

In an object-oriented database, the value of object attributes are only one method of referring to an object. The Employee objects could be inserted and retrieved using the emp_no contained in each object. Additionally, each object could be named and stored in the database under that name. Named identity becomes a problem when the number of objects stored becomes large. Finally, the system (program or database) could provide the identity of the object when the object is created without user input. This could be in a form that a user would find very difficult to work with, such as a large hexadecimal number. This would work well if the object identity procedures were independent of user interaction. All three methods of object identity require that the identifier be stored with or in the object.

Transparent Persistence

Transparent persistence is where the programming language provides the means to automatically maintain the object persistence. Many object-oriented database management systems provide a mechanism to implement transparent persistence. The Object Database Management Group (ODMG) developed class libraries to implement transparent persistence in C++ and Smalltalk. The implementation in Java is called Java Data Object (JDO). Although the ODMG completed its implementation in 2001 and was disbanded, it established the framework that is being implemented in all object-oriented languages. The concept of transparent persistence is that the application creates an object of type "persistent." Depending on the implementation, that may be inherited attributes. This object is placed in the database at creation. Each change is automatically updated in the database without the application having to manage it. Thus, the management of object persistence becomes the system's job, not the programmer's.

Storage and Access of Objects

The difference between object-oriented and relational databases is the way the data is stored. In a relational database, data is separated into normalized tables using data values, primary and foreign keys to maintain the data's relationships. In an object-oriented database, the object is stored and retrieved complete as an object. In the purest implementation, all the object's attributes would be stored with the object to include its methods. In reality, most of the methods are executed in the application so only the object state, or values, need to be stored. However, some database management systems will allow manipulation of the object from within the database. Any object method invoked inside the database must also be stored in the database.

```
employee(1005).giveRaise(1.1);
```

Sending the above code to the database would cause the database to execute the giveRaise method of the employee object identified by 1005. The object is modified within the database without the application having to retrieve it, update it, and store it back in the database.

One of the real advantages of object-oriented database management systems is the lack of impedance mismatch. Mapping the object's data to different data structures (as in a normalized relational schema) is referred to as impedance mismatch and it affects the performance of object retrieval. This is because the data must be mapped from the table structure to the object structure. Impedance mismatch is discussed in more detail in Chapter 7.

OBJECT-ORIENTED DESIGN

Object-oriented design is the process of defining the objects, their attributes and behaviors, and the interactions between the users and the objects. Because the database stores and retrieves whole objects, the steps required for data normalization are not used. The database design is determined in the design of the application objects. Primarily, the application design must determine the method of object identity that will be used, and if manually managed persistence or a form of transparent persistence will be implemented. This section discusses object-oriented design methods used in the application.

Object-Oriented Analysis

Object-oriented analysis starts with a traditional structured specification, and adds the following information:

- *A list of all objects:* A list describing the data contents of each *noun*, or physical entities in the data-flow diagrams (DFD).
- *A list all system behaviors:* A list of all *verbs* within the process, names such as *Prepare order* summary report, *generate* invoices, etc.
- *A list of the associated primary behaviors (services) with each object:* Each object will have behaviors that uniquely belong to the object. Other objects may request the behavior of the object.
- *A description of the contracts in the system:* A contract is an agreement between two objects, such that one object will invoke the services of the other.
- *A behavior script for each object:* A script describes each initiator, action, participant, and service.
- *A classification for each object and the object relationships:* Generate an entity-relationship (E-R) model and a generalization hierarchy (is-a) for each object, using traditional E-R or normalization techniques.

There are numerous books about different approaches to object analysis but they all contain these common elements. Now that we see the basic analysis requirements, we can explore the basic methodologies for object-oriented analysis.

Different Models for Object Analysis

Unlike the traditional systems analysis, where user requirements are gathered and then specifications are put on the requirements and users are then asked to sign off on the specifications, the object methodologies use a more iterative process where the requirements and specifications are reviewed repeatedly and the users are heavily involved.

Object technology has many different methodologies to help analyze and design computer systems. We review five of the more popular systems: (1) Rumbaugh, (2) Booch, (3) Coad–Yourdon, (4) Shlaer–Mellor, and (5) the Unified Modeling Language (UML). In most cases, these methodologies are very similar, but each has its own way of graphically representing the entities. To understand and use these four methodologies would become difficult, if not impossible, for all projects. If necessary, it is possible to use concepts from one method with concepts from another technique, basically creating your own object development technique. The most important point to remember is that the final outcome is what really matters, not the choice of one analysis technique over another. Remember that it is more important to do proper analysis and design to meet user requirements than it is to just follow a blind, meaningless procedure.

The traditional systems development approach is sometimes referred to as the waterfall method. By waterfall, object analysts follow a logical progression through analysis, design, coding, testing, and maintenance. Unfortunately system development seldom fits this kind of structured approach. End users are notorious for changing their minds or identifying some feature that they forgot to identify. These changes in requirements can happen at any phase of system development, and the analyst must struggle to accommodate these changes into the system. What it means to the systems analyst is that one must go back to whatever step in the development life cycle and make the necessary changes that will then cascade these changes through the entire system. For example, suppose that our end users are in the testing phase when they realize that they need an additional screen. This would require a change in the initial requirements document, which would, in turn, cascade to analysis, design, etc.

The object-oriented methodologies require a more iterative process with the same five steps. The iterative process either adds new or more clearly defines existing properties, unlike the traditional approach that would re-hash specifications that are already done. The iterative process helps reduce confusion surrounding what the system is really supposed to do and what the users really want. The object-oriented software development methods make the assumption that user requirements will change. However, it does not matter which programming language you use, be it Java or C++. Furthermore, it does not matter which system development technique you use; you will follow the same five steps in system development. It is just how these five steps are applied that will make the difference in your system development project.

The Rumbaugh Method

For traditional system analysts, the Rumbaugh methodology is closest to the traditional approach to system analysis and design, and beginners will recognize familiar symbols and techniques. The Rumbaugh methodology has its primary strength in object analysis, but it also does an excellent job with object design. Rumbaugh has three deliverables to the object analysis phase: (1) the object model, (2) the dynamic model, and (3) the functional model. These three models are similar to traditional system analysis, with some additions for the object model, including definitions of classes along with the class's variables and behaviors. The Rumbaugh object model is very much like an E-R diagram except that there are now behaviors in the diagram and class hierarchies. The dynamic model is a "state transition" diagram that shows how an entity changes from one state to another state. The functional model is the equivalent of the familiar data flow diagrams from a traditional systems analysis.

The Booch Method

Booch's methodology has its primary strength in the object system design. Grady Booch has included in his methodology a requirements analysis that is similar to a traditional requirements analysis, as well as a domain analysis phase. Booch's object system design method has four parts, the logical structure design where the class hierarchies are defined, and the physical structure diagram where the object methods are defined. Booch then defines the dynamics of classes in a fashion very similar to the Rumbaugh method, as well as an analysis of the dynamics of object instances, where he describes how an object can change state.

The Coad–Yourdon Method

Coad–Yourdon methodology has its primary strength in system analysis. This methodology is based on a technique called SOSAS, which stands for the five steps that help make up the analysis part of their methodology. The first step in system analysis is called "Subjects," which are basically data flow diagrams for objects. The second step is called "Objects," where they identify the object classes and the class hierarchies. The third step is called "Structures," where they decompose structures into two types: classification structures and composition structures. Classification structures handle the inheritance connection between related classes, while composition structures handle all the other connections among classes. The next step in analysis is called "Attributes," and the final step is called "Services," where all the behaviors or methods for each class are identified.

Following analysis, Coad and Yourdon define four parts that make up the design part of their methodology. The steps of system design are:

- *The problem domain component.* This will define the classes that should be in the problem domain.
- *The human interaction component.* These steps define the interface classes between objects.
- *The task management component.* This is where system-wide management classes are identified.
- *The data management component.* This design step identifies the classes needed for database access methods.

The Shlaer–Mellor Method

The Shlaer–Mellor methodology has its primary strength in system design and is considered somewhat weak on analysis. The Shlaer–Mellor methodology includes three models: (1) the information model, (2) the state model, and (3) the process model. The information model contains objects, variables, and all the relationships between the objects, and is basically a data model for the system. The state model records the different states of objects and changes that can occur between the objects, while the process model is really not much more than a traditional data flow diagram.

The Unified Modeling Language

In the mid-1990s, a company called Rational Software brought three of the main players (Booch, Rumbaugh, and Jacobson) together to create the Unified Modeling Language (UML). These three heavyweights in the area of object-oriented analysis and design created UML as a method of analyzing requirements, creating an effective design, and documenting the system. UML was accepted by the Object Management Group (OMG) in 1997 and continues to be refined. Almost all modern object-oriented programming tools have implemented at least part of the UML model into their development environments. Although UML is normally considered a notation model and a methodology, it is actually a notation that can be applied to almost all other methodologies.

UML tries to capture the details of a requirement and design so that they are clearly understood by the user, as well as the architect and the designer. It captures both static and dynamic relationships between objects. UML consists of the following diagrams:

- *Use case diagrams.* Use case diagrams capture the interaction between actors in implementing a single action within the program.

A requirements document will contain many use cases, defining all the user interactions within the program.

- *Class diagrams.* These diagrams show static relationships between groups of classes. They show class inheritance, containment, and dependencies.
- *Object diagrams.* These diagrams show relationships between classes in a given point in time or state.
- *StateChart diagrams.* These diagrams capture dynamic relationships and define how objects change state or attributes.
- *Activity diagrams.* These diagrams show how behaviors flow in the system and interact within each object's state. They are similar to a flow diagram defining the workflow between objects.
- *Interaction diagrams.* These diagrams model system behavior, and include both Sequence diagrams and Collaboration diagrams.
- *Component diagrams.* These diagrams characterize the physical makeup of the system, place objects into components (files, etc.), and define the interaction between those components.
- *Deployment diagrams.* These diagrams define how the finished system is architected, including relationships and processes.

As one can see, UML is a complete modeling system — from analysis to deployment. There are a number of books dedicated to UML, along with numerous Web sites. Search on UML or try the OMG Web site (www.omg.org) or the Rational Web site (www.rational.com).

CREATING THE OBJECT MODEL

The object model is one of the three main models used to describe the complete logical processing in the system. The object model will include the basic object elements, the objects behaviors (methods), the data attributes (variables), and how one object relates to another object. The object model is essentially a graphical roadmap for the system and is an extremely useful tool for both the developers as well as the end-user community. An object's behaviors and variables are listed inside the object boxes, and the object relationships with other objects are designated by the lines connecting the boxes. The object model can be extremely helpful when questions or concerns arise, because one can visually see the design of the system and how the system is constructed.

The object model is also the basis for the database design. In the object model, objects that require persistence are identified and a method for object identity is defined. Depending on the capabilities of the object-oriented database management system that will be used with the project, additional attributes may need to be publicly accessible to improve object

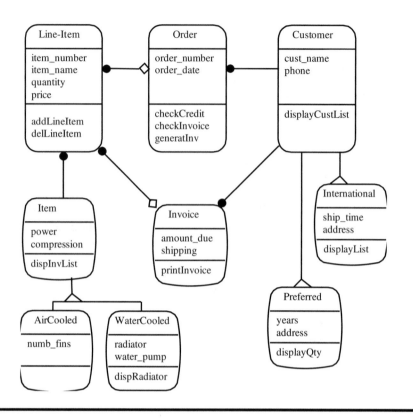

Figure 6.1 An object model for an order processing system.

retrieval. For example, if we need to retrieve all employee objects with the last name "SMITH," the database must be able to access the attribute last_name. Placing an index on the last_name attribute may also improve performance. These factors depend on the capabilities and requirements of the database management system used to implement the persistent storage.

The object model is a close cousin of the entity-relationship (E-R) diagram. In fact, the object model is sometimes referred to as an entity-relationship model with the additional constructs of classes and behaviors.

For example, if we are trying to develop an ordering system for a business, it might look like the object model in Figure 6.1. This figure is an object model for Earl's Engines, a small manufacturer of engines for riding lawn mowers.

Let us examine the meaning of the symbols in the object model diagram, starting with the rectangles. The rectangle contains three areas: the class name, the data attributes (values) in the class, and the methods that participate in the class.

The core of the object model consists of the class entities. For Earl's Engines, we see both the base classes and subclasses for the model. The base classes include Line-Item, Order, Customer, Invoice, and Item. The subclasses include Preferred, International, AirCooled, and WaterCooled (see Figure 6.1). As one might guess, the Line-Item data attributes would be item_number, item_name, quantity, and price. The class behaviors follow the class attributes, and we see that in the Line-Item class they are listed as addLineItem and delLineItem.

Let us now examine the nature of the lines that connect the objects. In Figure 6.1, the dark circles seen on the lines represent the many sides of a one-to-many relationship. For example, we see that there is a one-to-many relationship between a customer and an order, because a customer can place many orders, but each order belongs to only one customer. The diamond-shaped symbols represent aggregation. For example, we see that an order is an aggregation of many line items. Finally, we see the triangle-shaped junction that represents subclasses. For example, we see that a customer has two subclasses, one for Preferred customers and another for International customers. These subclasses are used to show the new data items and methods that are unique to the subclass.

Now take a closer look at aggregation. For example, the order-request entity is an aggregate entity made up of many Line-Items, but each Line-Item has only one order. The diamond symbol seen on the Invoice class and the Order class is used to denote an aggregation of a number of things (aggregations are sometimes referred to as collections, or assembles). Here we see that an Order object is made up of an aggregation of many Line-Items plus one Customer object. An invoice is an aggregation of many Line-Items plus one Customer object.

Note: We are deliberately using the terms "class" and "entity" interchangeably. To the object model, they both denote a definition of an object, and the reader should become accustomed to these synonymous terms.

The object model for Earl's Engines also represents is-a class hierarchies between classes. We use the term "is-a" because that is how we specify the participation option of subclasses. For example, a Dodge minivan is-a van, a van is-a car, and a car is-a vehicle. For Earl, the Customer class has two subclasses, a Preferred customer and an International customer, each with its own data and behaviors, such that a Preferred customer is-a customer and an International customer is-a customer. We also see a class hierarchy in the Item object, where we see AirCooled and Water-Cooled subtypes for the Item.

In short, the object model describes all the relationships between entities, the class hierarchies that exist for each entity, and the methods for each class.

In this example, the bold objects need to be persistent. Item, Line-Item, Order, Customer, and Invoice will make up parts of our database schema. Because we are not linking these objects together with foreign keys, we will have to implement some method of linking the objects together. In the object model, the Order object has a one-to-many relationship to the Line-Item object. In the physical design, this can be implemented by adding a collection of Line-Item objects to the Order object. With this implementation, the Line-Item object does not need an attribute for object identity because the actual Line-Item objects will be contained in the Order object.

Note: this is an example of how object-oriented databases violate normalization. Each object contains all of its Line-Item objects, possibly introducing significant redundancy of data in the database. However, retrieving the Order object is significantly easier because the object is stored as a whole and not created by joining tables.

The Customer object also has a one-to-many relationship with the Order object. However, in the physical model, we decide not to place the Order object in the Customer object. This decision was made because the Customer object is used by many other parts of our application so we wanted to separate the actual Order objects from its Customer object. In our design, each Order object has a unique order_number attribute (called order) that can be used for object identity. One method of implementation would be to place a collection of order_numbers as an attribute to the Customer object. However, because an order has only one customer, it would be easier to place the customer identity into the Order object. For this we need a unique object identity for the Customer object, which we will call the customer number or cust_num.

Finally, we want to manipulate orders only through the Customer object so we need to build in the methods for retrieving and manipulating Order objects in the Customer object. We can add a behavior or method to the Customer object to retrieve all customer orders and one to retrieve the most recent customer order.

In Figure 6.2, the Order object now contains a collection of Line-Items and the customer number. The Customer object contains methods to access and manipulate the orders belonging to that customer. The schema has been implemented at containing the objects Item, Line-Item, Order, Invoice, and Customer. Although not discussed, an analysis of the Invoice object is also necessary.

METHODS AND DATABASE OBJECTS

In a pure object-oriented implementation, the object methods are stored in the database with the object. Most database management systems store

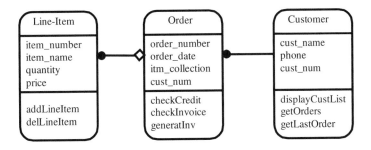

Figure 6.2 Physical model of Order and Customer objects.

the methods separate from the data and many do not store methods at all. There are three implementation of object methods relating to the database: (1) application maintained methods, (2) database maintained methods, and (3) database executed methods.

Most object-oriented programs define the methods in the class definitions for that object. In this case, it is appropriate to not store the object's methods because the object is retrieved first into an object of the appropriate type that contains the methods. This is an example of application methods. In this instance, the program maintains the behavior definitions and the database stores the object state.

In the implementation of database method definitions, the database maintains both the state and the behavior. The application only needs to know what methods it can call, not how they are defined. The program retrieves an object from the database into an object type. It then calls the object method to change the state of the object.

```
object obj = new object;
obj := retrieve employee where emp_num=2004;
obj.giveRaise(1.1);
update(obj);
```

In the above pseudo code, we create a generic object. We retrieve the Employee object that has the identity of 2004. We then execute the giveRaise method and update the object in the database. We actually knew nothing about the object except that it had a giveRaise method and that we wanted to execute that method on the retrieved object.

The final implementation is a mixture of application and database methods. By having methods for use by the application and methods executed in the database, one can achieve higher performance at the expense of increased complexity and maintenance. For example, our application normally retrieves objects and then manipulates them. However, some behavior changes do not require that the object be read into memory to execute. In this case, the application can call the database to have the method executed by the database. For example, if one is going to give TOM a raise, it is not a problem to retrieve the object TOM and execute the method. However, if one is giving all employees a raise, it will be much more efficient to call the giveRaise method for each Employee object and skip the requirement for retrieval and update. There are other benefits, in that the database administrator may be able to optimize the code executing inside the database. The problem is that the application developer must in many cases maintain two sets of code, one in the application and another in the database. Changing the application code without updating the database code may corrupt the data.

SUMMARY

This chapter introduced the concepts of object-oriented programming and object-oriented databases. Unlike relational databases, the design of the program determines the design of the database. Objects created in the application can either be persistent or transient. Persistent objects must be placed in the database, either programmatically or by implementing a form of transparent persistence.

Object-oriented databases can provide significant performance advantages to applications that manipulate complex data as a whole; however, they are not suited for applications that manipulate data in small amounts by multiple access methods.

Chapter 7 takes the object-oriented program and maps it to the relational database using the object-relational models.

7

OBJECT-RELATIONAL
DESIGN

Designing a relational database schema that interacts with an object-oriented language is more difficult than it first appears. As gleaned from Chapter 6, object-oriented languages hold data in objects that consist of the data and the methods to support the data. In a relational database, the data is normalized to support efficient storage and access. The application creates an object that contains collections of data and processes the data as an object. The data in one object can map to multiple tables and possibly multiple databases. The problems encountered when mapping an object-oriented language, such as Java or C++, to a declarative language, like SQL, are called impedance mismatch. Impedance mismatch is caused by the fact that one object in the application can contain data from multiple tables and multiple rows within a table, as seen in Figure 7.1.

This makes the conversion from object data to normalized database table data problematic. In an object-oriented database, as discussed in Chapter 6, objects are created, inserted, updated, and deleted as an object. In an object-relational database, one must map that object into a normalized relational database and each of those steps may then require multiple SQL statements. To reduce the effect of impedance mismatch, modern database management systems have implemented some object-oriented features such as user-defined datatypes, object identity, and encapsulated member methods.

This chapter relates to topics discussed in Chapter 6, "Object-Oriented Database Design." Both the object-oriented and object-relational database schema designs are heavily influenced by program design. Trying to design the database schema without knowing the definition of the application's persistent objects will result in greater impedance mismatch. Therefore, either the application and database must be developed together or the application objects should be designed first.

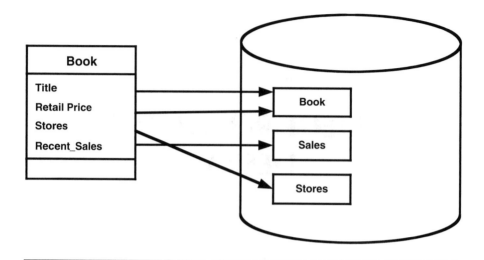

Figure 7.1   Impedance mismatch.

ADVANTAGES OF OBJECT-RELATIONAL DATABASES

One of the important drawbacks of a pure object-oriented database is that the data is stored and accessed as an object. Querying internal data elements is difficult, if possible at all. Ad hoc querying capability is difficult to implement and complicated to use. This drawback is one of the strengths of the object-relational database.

Atomic, Normalized Data

Because the object data is stored in relational tables, the data is accessible through SQL queries. This allows easy aggregation or manipulation of individual pieces of data. However, the data is not necessarily normalized to the same extent that a purely relational database schema would be. Object-relational databases attempt to have the best of both worlds: object access and functionality with SQL access of data to the granular level. Although not perfect at either, the object-relational database is quite successful at achieving both goals.

Ad hoc Queries

Because the data is stored in relational tables, it is possible to query data elements that normally would be internal to an object. The Employee object may contain a data element called emp_state. This piece of data may be stored in a user-defined datatype called address that contains the full mailing address of the employee. One can query all the employee numbers from the state of Colorado by reading each address record and discarding those with an address.emp_state not equal to "CO." This ability is a significant improvement over purely object-oriented databases.

The first step is to define what object-oriented features the object database management system implements that allow it to blend object requirements to the flexibility of the relational schema. To start, we discuss the object type.

OBJECT TYPES

The introduction of object types in the relational database allows one to create user-defined types from any other defined type with the database. The metadata defining the datatype is also available to the application.

```
CREATE OR REPLACE TYPE   full_mailing_address_type
AS OBJECT
( Street          VARCHAR2(80),
  City            VARCHAR2(80),
  State           CHAR(2),
  Zip             VARCHAR2(10) );
```

In the above example, we created an object type called full_mailing_address_type that contains the complete mailing address of an entity. Once defined, one can create a table using the new datatype:

```
CREATE TABLE customer
    ( cust_id              varchar2(8),
      cust_name            varchar2(80),
      full_address         full_mailing_address_type,
    );
```

The ANSI SQL standard has been extended to allow access to user-defined objects and datatypes; however, each database management system currently implements objects in its own manner, so all the object features are not available in every database or may be implemented in a unique way. One should refer to the database vendor's documentation. Once the table has been created (see Figure 7.2), it can be manipulated using SQL.

```
insert into customer values
(  'C0104',
   'Samuel Spade'
   full_mailing_address_type ('123 This
St','HereIn','CO','80406')
);
```

cust_id	cust_name	full_address			
		Street	City	State	Zip

Figure 7.2 Customer table definition.

Selecting the address using SQL is just as easy. Notice that the complex datatype full_address is copied as an object into v_address. The application can then access the internal data elements of v_address:

```
v_address    full_mailing_address_type;
v_street     varchar2(80);

select full_address
into v_address
from customer
where cust_id ='C0104';

v_street := v_address.street;
```

As one can see in the example above, access to internal data is obtained by using the "." dot notation. Objects are based on the class object in object-oriented languages, such as C++ and Java. As we will see, database objects can also encapsulate object methods to manipulate the object data. And, similar to objects in an object-oriented database management system, objects in some object-relational databases can support inheritance and polymorphism.

Another feature of the object type is that it can encapsulate member methods. This would allow an application to execute a method on the database server to obtain some result, rather than instantiating the object on the client, reading the object from the database, and then executing the class member method.

```
CREATE TYPE employee as object
(  emp_number        number,
   emp_last_name     varchar2(80),
   emp_first_name    varchar2(60),
   emp_hire_date     date,
   emp_salary        number,
   emp_address       full_mailing_address_type,
   emp_department    varchar2(20),
   emp_title         varchar2(30),
   emp_manager       number,
   map member function get_name return varchar2,
   not final;
);
```

In the example above, we created an object that contained not only data, but also a function called "get_name." Below we define the function:

```
CREATE TYPE BODY employee AS
  map member function get_name return number is
  begin
    return emp_last_name||',  '||emp_first_name;
  end;
end;
```

The member function get_name will return the employee's last and first names. One could call this method using SQL:

```
SELECT e.get_name() FROM employee e;
```

The encapsulating member method in the database is a powerful feature but must be used with care. The encapsulated member method itself is not returned with the object and is only applicable to the object in the database. If the application retrieves an object to the client side for processing and then calls the member method, the object in the client no longer matches the object in the database because the encapsulated member only applied to the object in the database. This feature can result in invalid data between the application and the database.

Not all object-relational databases support inheritance. If your database does, it will allow you to derive subtypes from an already-defined type. If supported, the subtype may add attributes or methods to those inherited from the original type. The subtype may also be allowed to redefine methods inherited from the original type, called polymorphism.

```
CREATE TYPE manager UNDER employee (
  mag_level    NUMBER,
  mag_title    VARCHAR2(30))
NOT FINAL;
```

In the example above, we have created a subtype of employee called manager. This was possible because the employee type contains the NOT FINAL clause. The manager type inherits all the attributes and methods contained in the employee type, and adds two attributes (Figure 7.3). Because the manager type is not final, one could create a subtype of manager — for example, a vice_pres type.

Large Objects

Another object implemented is the large object (LOB). Large objects are used to store large amounts of binary or text data. LOBs can be stored

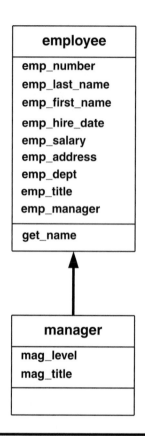

Figure 7.3   Inheritance in a subtype.

internally in the database or externally in operating system files. A CLOB is a large character object, while a BLOB is a large binary object. Internally, CLOBs are BLOBs with additional methods defined to support text. Using LOBs allows one to simply place an object in the data; it does not necessarily allow one to do anything with it. For example, one might want to place a large text document into a CLOB in the database. One creates a table called "documents" containing a document key, document name, and a CLOB to actually store the document. Once the document is loaded into the database, one can reference the CLOB by the document key. The ANSI SQL3 standard does not provide any additional help in manipulating the data inside the CLOB. However, different database management systems will provide non-standard capabilities, such as the ability to index the text within the CLOB. These capabilities are proprietary and will be implemented differently, depending on which database product is used. BLOBs are similar to CLOBs, except that they hold binary data. This could be a compressed file, a compiled program, or a picture.

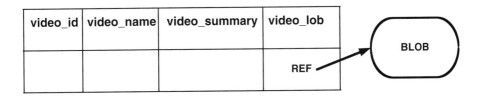

Figure 7.4   Binary large objects.

The data is just a group of bits stored within the database. Finally, the standard also defines an NCLOB as a special CLOB that holds national characters or 2-byte characters.

Large objects are routinely used to store and manipulate large items that internally cannot be indexed or identified. Multimedia items, such as streaming sound and video, can be maintained within the database as one column in a table with the identification information stored in another column:

```
CREATE TABLE video_store (
    video_id        NUMBER,
    video_name      varchar2(80),
    video_summary   varchar2(1000),
    video_lob       BLOB
);
```

The above example creates a table called "video_store" that contains videos. The actual video is stored in the database as a BLOB, as shown in Figure 7.4.

The database can search for videos by name, id number, or by searching for keywords in the summary text. This provides an effective way to locate a specific BLOB, although the BLOB itself does not contain that information.

Collections

Collections provide the ability to store and process groups of related data. There are two collections stored in the database: (1) the variable array and (2) the nested table. Arrays are part of the ANSI SQL3 standard, but nested tables are an extension provided by the database vendor. Again, implementation of these features varies between database vendors.

Arrays

Arrays allow a collection of objects to be stored in a table column. Although implementation varies among database management systems, for the most

player name	player name	player name	player name	player name	player name	player name	player name

Figure 7.5 Array objects.

part, arrays have a defined or "max" size and are manipulated as an object (Figure 7.5). They are inserted, updated, etc. as a complete object, rather than separate elements within an object. As such, they are not sparse, meaning that they cannot contain empty elements. Arrays can contain standard datatypes or abstract datatypes. The only requirement is that all elements are the same type. Creating an array is similar to creating other object types.

```
CREATE OR REPLACE TYPE  player_array
AS  VARRAY(10) OF varchar2(80);

CREATE TABLE team
(  team_name              varchar(40),
   team_sport             varchar2(40),
   team_players           player_array
 );
```

Once created, the array is manipulated as an object:

```
NSERT INTO team values
( 'TIGERS',
  'BASEBALL',
  team_players('Tom Smith','Sam Spade','Joan Hearts')
);

v_tm_members team_players;

SELECT team_players INTO v_tm_members
FROM team
WHERE team_name = 'TIGERS';
```

Nested Tables

While an array allows one to place a defined number of elements as a table column, the nested table allows a table to be created as a table

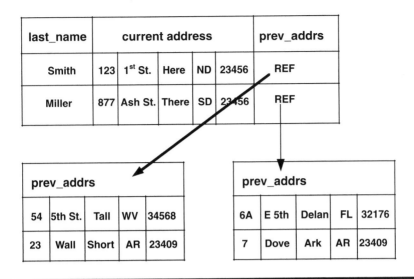

last_name	current address					prev_addrs
Smith	123	1st St.	Here	ND	23456	REF
Miller	877	Ash St.	There	SD	23456	REF

prev_addrs				
54	5th St.	Tall	WV	34568
23	Wall	Short	AR	23409

prev_addrs				
6A	E 5th	Delan	FL	32176
7	Dove	Ark	AR	23409

Figure 7.6 Nested tables.

column. A nested table is used when there is a large number of data elements that are not stored in sequence and can be changed independent of the other data contained in the nested table. Nested tables are sparse, which means that one can delete rows within the nested table. While arrays are normally stored inline — in the actual row of data — nested tables are normally implemented by placing a reference in the data row that points to the nested table, as in Figure 7.6.

Creating a nested table is not difficult; manipulating the data in the nested table, however, can be complicated.

```
CREATE OR REPLACE TYPE full_mailing_address_type
AS OBJECT
( Street          VARCHAR2(80),
  City            VARCHAR2(80),
  State           CHAR(2),
  Zip             VARCHAR2(10)
);

CREATE TYPE prev_addrs AS OBJECT
( prior_address          full_mailing_address_type);

CREATE TYPE nested_address AS TABLE OF prev_addrs;
```

After creating the nested table, we can place it into a table as a column:

```
CREATE TABLE emp1
( last_name            char(40),
  current_address      full_mailing_address_type,
  prev_address         nested_address)
  NESTED TABLE prev_address
  STORE AS prev_address_nt;
```

Manipulating the data in a nested table depends on the database system being used.

```
SELECT   last_name, e.current_address.state,
  s.prev_address.state
FROM emp1 e, TABLE(e.prev_address) s;

--------------
Heart   CO   VA
Heart   CO   NC
Heart   CO   AR
Heart   CO   AK
```

A final note on nested tables: most implementations will create a separate table connected to the original table by a *foreign key* instead of implementing a nested table. This provides easier access to the individual data elements that would be stored inside the nested table. However, if the application reads the nested table as an object, one will not be able to use the foreign key implementation.

OBJECT VIEWS

An object view is a virtual object table in which each object is represented as a row. Like a normal view that can be used to join tables to create a virtual table, the object view collects data from the relational tables to build the complex datatypes of the object.

Using an object view, one can fetch object data to the persistent layer and map it into language classes for use by the application. The application is insulated from the complexity of taking the relational tables and creating the objects. Another advantage is that as application development continues, changes in objects can quickly be implemented in the database by redefining the object view.

```
CREATE TABLE author (
    author_key     NUMBER (5),
    author_name    VARCHAR2 (20),
    author_add     full_add_type
);
```

```
CREATE TYPE author_t AS OBJECT (
    author_key      NUMBER (5),
    author_name     VARCHAR2 (20),
    author_add      full_add_type
);


CREATE VIEW auth_view1 OF author_t
    WITH OBJECT IDENTIFIER (author_key) AS
        SELECT a.author_key,
               a.author_name,
               a.author_add
           FROM author a;
```

The above example simply takes the author table and creates an object view of the data in the table. Normally, the object view would pull data from multiple tables.

So far, we have introduced the object-relational features implemented in modern database management systems. The examples used above follow Oracle's implementation, but were as generic as possible. Because each vendor implements these features uniquely, one will need to determine the capabilities of the database one is using and how difficult is it to implement the object features. Understand that once the application is developed, changing to a database from another vendor may cause significant problems in porting the application. Once one has determined the object features one is going to implement, be flexible and test. During development, one may find that a feature is available but does not perform at the level required to support the application. Test the capability before locking in the design.

USING LOGICAL POINTERS

Before beginning a discussion of pointers, it is important to understand exactly what a pointer represents and how it is implemented in object databases. In pre-relational databases, each record in the database had a distinct address. These addresses were the numbers that corresponded to a physical database block. Also included in the address was the "offset" or displacement of the target record into the block. For example, an address of 665:2 would refer to the second record in database block number 665. Once defined, these addresses could be stored inside other records, essentially allowing one record to point to another record. These pointers became the foundation for establishing relationships between entities in pre-relational times.

For the object-relational databases, there is the ability to create a distinct object identifier (OID) to uniquely identify each row within an object-relational table. These OIDs are guaranteed to remain unique by the database software, and like pointers, OIDs can be embedded into columns, providing the ability to point to other rows in the database.

Although the design of pointer-based databases was very elegant in the sense that foreign keys were not needed to establish data relationships, there were serious problems with implementation. Network databases such as CA-IDMS and hierarchical databases such as IMS are very difficult to navigate because the programmer must be aware of the location, name, and types of each pointer in the database.

Even worse, the use of pointers for establishing data relationships makes structural changes a nightmare. Because the data relationships are "hard linked" with embedded pointers, the addition of a new pointer requires special utility programs to "sweep" each and every affected entity in the database. As each record is located, the prefix of the entity is restructured to accommodate the new pointers. While the "pure" object-oriented databases have this problem of restructuring, the object-relational databases avoid this problem because the SQL ALTER TABLE syntax can be used to add the new pointer column to the entity without restructuring all the rows in the table.

One major feature of the relational database model is their requirement that rows be addressed by the contents of their data values (with the exception of relational databases that support the ROW_ID construct). Now, within the object-relation model, there will be an alternative access method for rows, such that rows can be identified by either their data values or by their OIDs. For example:

```
SELECT
      customer_stuff
FROM
      customer
WHERE
      customer_ID = 38373;
```

In the object-relational model, we can also use SQL to address rows by their OIDs, thereby allowing pointer-based database navigation:

```
SELECT
      customer_stuff
FROM
      customer
WHERE
   OID = :host_variable;
```

A navigational programmer is required to clearly describe the access path that the database will use to service the request. The access path is clearly described in their code, and programmers can graphically show the path with an object-relational diagram (as described in Chapter 3). In SQL, however, the access path in not evident and is hidden because the access is determined by the SQL optimizer, usually at runtime. The SQL optimizer interrogates the system tables to see if the "target" relational tables have indexes, an then determines the optimal access path to service the SQL request. The SQL optimizer uses several access methods, including sequential scans, sequential pre-fetch, and index scans.

Using pointers will allow the designer to define and implement "aggregate objects" that contain pointer references to the components, rather than having to define a relational view on the data. This will also allow the database designer to more effectively model the real world, reduce overhead, and also provide a way to attach "methods" or behaviors to aggregate objects.

Now take a look at how repeating values appear in the object-relational model. The database language uses the varying-array language construct (VARRAY) introduced earlier to indicate repeating groups, so we can use the VARRAY mechanism to declare repeating groups within table columns. Let us examine an example. In the following SQL, we add a repeating group called book title to our author table. First we create an object TYPE called book_title with a maximum of three values:

```
CREATE TYPE auth_name (
      first_name          char(30),
      middle_initial      char(1),
      last_name           char(40));

 CREATE TYPE full_address (
      street_address      char(60),
      city_address        char(40),
      state_name          char(2),
      zip_code            char(9));

 CREATE TYPE book_title (
      pub_date            Date,
      publisher_name      char(80),
      book_title          char(80)
      book_isbn           full_address);

 CREATE TYPE book_history (
      VARRAY(3) OF REF book_title);
```

Note that the VARRAY does not contain book_title objects but references (REF) to book_title objects. Now that we have defined the datatypes, here is how we can create the object-relational table using the datatypes:

```
CREATE TABLE AUTHOR (
        author_name        full_name,
        auth_address       full_address,
        book_data          book_history);

CREATE TABLE BOOK_HISTORY (
        Book_details       book_title);
```

Notice that the there is no foreign key relating the book information in the book_history table to the authors in the author table. That reference is supplied by the pointers in the VARRAY for each author.

Using SQL to retrieve the data simply requires dereferencing the VARRAY value we need.

```
SELECT author.book_data.book_title(2)
From AUTHOR
WHERE author.author_name.last_name = 'SPADE';
```

Also note that if we have multiple authors writing one book we will end up with duplicate records in the book_history table. This of course violates first normal form. One of the issues associated with using object-relational mapping is that the relational scheme will normally violate first normal form. However, this is not normally a problem because the application will access and manipulate the data as a whole object rather than at the smallest data element, normal for relational database applications.

To establish data relationships between database entities, a pointer must be persistent, unique, and non-expiring. In pre-object-relational databases, a relational Row ID was used to identify a row. Unfortunately, this Row ID was the number of the physical database block and row displacement within the data block. As such, a relational row could "move" to another block as a result of routine maintenance, or be deleted. To address this problem, the object-relational vendors have devised a way to create OIDs for each row that will always uniquely identify a row, regardless of the row's status. For example, a database row could be deleted, and the OID that was associated with that row will never be reused by the database software.

In a traditional relational database, we could create the table as follows:

```
CREATE TABLE author (author_data        author_info);
```

With the introduction of OIDs, the table creation syntax has changed slightly. The following example will create the exact same table as our earlier example, with the exception that the table will contain an OID for each row that is created within the customer table:

```
CREATE TABLE author OF author_info;
```

Now, using the database's ability to nest or embed a table in a table, we can create a table containing aggregate objects.

```
CREATE TYPE book_info
   AS TABLE OF book_title;   --from prev. example

CREATE TYPE author_info (
    author_id            integer,
    author_full_name     full_name,
    author_full_address  full_address,
    book_list            book_info);

CREATE TABLE author OF author_info;
```

In the first command, we create an object type that is a table of book_title types defined in the previous example. Remember that this creates a type definition, not an actual table. In the second command, we create an object type with four elements, three of which are defined object types. In the last command, we actually create a physical table in the database with one column, the author_info type, containing a nested table of book_info types. This table could hold the entire application author object (if it was designed with the same items), to include the list of books written by the author.

Using pointers can also become overly complicated when one requires the ability to select within the nested objects. If one is looking for a list of book_titles, sorted by publishing data, one will require a pretty complicated query. In cases where persistent object data is accessed outside the object definition, one should map the data into "more" normalized database tables to allow for more efficient, non-object access. As discussed earlier, a decision to implement pointers in the database design is defined by the design of the application. If the application does not create objects that reference internal objects as pointers, one will probably not want to try and implement pointer references in the database.

COMPARISON OF OBJECT-ORIENTED AND OBJECT-RELATIONAL DATABASES

Chapter 6 introduced the object-oriented database, which provides object persistence to object-oriented languages. This chapter discusses the object-relational database, which is a relational database that implements object types to support object-oriented applications. Finally, there is the purely relational database, which has no direct support for object types. Although object-oriented and object-relational databases are the newcomers to the field, they have been around for a number of years and are mature, capable systems. Most enterprise-level database management systems support either object-oriented or object-relational features.

The declarative nature of SQL provides good access to data and is highly optimized in today's databases; however, it is not able to efficiently handle complex datatypes embedded in today's object-oriented applications. The object-oriented databases handle persistence of objects easily (complex data objects) but have significant problems accessing internal data, not as an object. The object-relational features added to the relational database improve SQL performance by defining and manipulating complex datatypes as objects.

As today's enterprise database management systems continue to advance, the line between the three types is beginning to blur and the performance advantage of one type of database over another is disappearing. This has given rise to the term "universal database server." All vendors would like you to believe that a universal server is now available, but the reality is that there is further progress needed for that to be true.

CREATING THE OBJECT-RELATIONAL DESIGN

When talking about logical design, one normally tries to avoid moving into the physical design; but when designing an object to be stored in a relational database, one must consider the capabilities of the database management system one is using and the object features one feels comfortable implementing. Having determined which features will be used, one can then move toward a design. At this point we assume that the application is an object-oriented design and that one is using an object-relational database as the persistent storage. In this section we are going to cross into discussing the physical design of the database.

The term most often used in moving from the object-oriented application design to the object-relational database is "mapping." Objects are mapped to the normalized (or partially normalized) data in relational tables. This mapping usually involves the following steps:

1. Review the object navigation and create logical pointers.
2. Add object extensions to manage internal pointers.
3. For each class, map the data items and pointers to a relational table.
4. Write C/Java/SQL snippets to move the object data and pointers into the table row.
5. Rewrite the I/O to utilize the logical pointers.

Logical Object Pointers

The usage of pointers to navigate object relationships within a traditional object-oriented application may also have to be reworked if one plans to use a relational database. In a nonpersistent C++ application, an object is created with the NEW operator, memory is allocated, and the address of that object is captured. Of course, this address is not permanent, and a subsequent run of the application may find the same object in another memory address. For this reason, a method must be determined to replace the "physical" memory address pointers with "logical" pointers to the object. This logical pointer is the object identity (discussed in detail in Chapter 6).

The question of access to relational data is simplified if we mark a data item as being the primary key for the object. In this fashion, we can always retrieve the object from disk using SQL and place in a re-instantiated object.

The next question is how to map complex attribute such as collections contained in the object. Collections can be mapped to a set of rows in a child table but the object key must be added to map the rows back to the parent object. Once all the attributes are mapped to tables, it is a simple process to create the SQL to stuff them in the tables of the database. Of course, the relational table will not be able to make any sense of these pointers, and the relational table structure would not contain any of the "foreign keys" that we are accustomed to using for relational navigation. SQL joins cannot be used against these tables, but queries against individual tables can still be performed.

Consider the following example. Here we have one customer, TOM, who has two orders, order 123 and order 456. The customer object will have collections of pointers to orders, and will store the in-memory pointers for order 123 and order 456. Each order, in turn, will store a pointer to customer TOM.

Next, we want to make these objects persistent and store them as rows in our relational database. We want to store customer TOM as a row in the customer table, and orders 123 and 456 will each store as rows in the order table. Because we will store "TOM" as the primary key for the customer and as a foreign key for each order, we can be assured that the logical relationship between these relational rows will be maintained.

But what happens when customer TOM is retrieved by a subsequent run of our application? We can easily use SQL to retrieve the customer row from the table and instantiate the object for customer ABC, but how can we establish the pointers to orders 123 and 456? They have not yet been retrieved, and will not have addresses until we manually call them in from the database and re-instantiate them. At this point, customer TOM's

array of pointers to orders contains nothing but NULL pointers, because the orders have not been retrieved from memory. However, we could write a routine that would check to see if the pointer is NULL, and then go to the database and retrieve all orders for the customer with an SQL statement. In this case, we know that each order is identified by a unique order number, but it may not always be so easy to find a key for the sub-objects. However, because we store the order rows with the customer object identity (TOM), we can retrieve the row containing the customer key, instantiate it into order objects, and load the objects (actually pointers) into the orders collection in the TOM customer object.

A review shows that an order object contains one to many line-item objects. Again, these line-item objects must be factored into a relational table with a key back to the order object identity. The order object must now have a method for storing, updating, and retrieving the line-item objects that belong to it.

Now that we have mapped the object data to table rows, we need to ensure that the object state is always stored in the database. It is the application's responsibility to ensure that changes made to the object's state are updated to the object data stored in the database. A persistent object must be able to survive the crash of the application. Each method that changes the object's state must be updated to write that change to the database. In this way, the database stays up-to-date with each object's state.

Finally, methods must be created that handle object-to-database I/O. These include loading newly instantiated objects into the database and the ability to delete objects from the database. This code may be included as part of the object itself for part of the application code.

Although the concept is rather simple, the execution of mapping objects and relational tables can become overwhelming. Luckily, there are a number of tools on the market to assist in mapping objects to relational tables.

Automated Tools

Because most object-oriented applications use a relational database for persistence storage, a number of tools have been developed to assist in the object-to-relational mapping. These tools do all the hard work for you. For example, they can take the objects defined in the application and not only map them into relational tables (the tool will define the tables), but also generate the code necessary to manage the storage and retrieval of the object data. Most can also map existing application objects to existing relational tables and generate any additional tables needed to maintain object identity. All these tools work with specific object-oriented languages, such as Java or C++, but most will work with any relational database.

SUMMARY

This chapter discussed the use of relational databases to provide persistence to object-oriented applications. In recent years, relational database management systems have implemented many object features, such as abstract datatypes and collections; however, many of these items are database-vendor-specific in capability and implementation. Mapping objects to relational tables depends on defining the object identity in a form that can be used as a key in the relational tables. Finally, persistence must be updated as the object state changes to ensure that the object state survives the ending or crash of the application.

8

DESIGNING
REPLICATED DATABASES

Database replication is the copying of part or all of a database to one or more remote sites. The remote site can be in another part of the world, or right next to the primary site. Because of the speed and reliability of the Internet, many people believe that database replication is no longer needed. While it is true that distributed transactions provide access to real-time data almost anywhere in the world, they require that all databases operate all the time. When one database is down for any reason or cannot be contacted, other databases can no longer access its data. Replication solves this problem because each site has a copy of the data.

When a query accesses data on multiple databases, it is called a *distributed query*. Applications using distributed queries are difficult to optimize because each brand (in fact, different versions of the same brand) of database handles the execution of the query differently. Sometimes, the local database will retrieve data from the remote database and process it locally. This can result in high network bandwidth use and slow query performance. More modern databases will analyze the query and send a request to the remote database for only that information it needs — greatly reducing network traffic, but also making performance tuning very complicated. Either way, distributed queries always contain some network latency time. If this response delay becomes unacceptable, replicating the databases may be the solution. Querying local data is always faster than accessing remote data.

Replication of all or part of a database is becoming increasingly common as companies consolidate servers and information. Many companies use some form of replication to load data into the company data warehouse. It can also be used to create a separate database for reporting, thereby removing the impact of data aggregation from the main database. Many companies use replication to create a subset of data that is accessed by another application, a Web site for example. By replicating only a subset of the data, or using non-updateable replication, they can protect sensitive information while allowing users to have access to up-to-date data.

Replication is also used in high-availability databases that require zero-failover times. An application can re-query the replicated database if it receives an error from the primary database. Modern databases can sometimes determine that a transaction has failed and automatically re-query the alternate database. Having multiple databases maintaining the same data also allows users to be load balanced.

Database replication does have limitations, and understanding those limitations can ensure that a replication project is successful.

This chapter introduces database replication and discusses planning and design considerations. Because enterprise database systems each have their own methods of implementing replication, this chapter avoids the detail of the actual construction and focuses on the available methods.

MANUAL REPLICATION TECHNIQUES

The simplest form of replication just creates a copy of a table on another database. This can be done using whatever technique the database implements for moving data in or out of a database. For example, most databases have utilities to export data to an operating system file and other utilities to import that file into another database. Data can also be moved from one database to another using a distributed query such as:

```
CREATE TABLE emp AS
SELECT
   Emp_name,
   Emp_address
   Emp_key
FROM
   emp@primary_database
WHERE
      Emp_dept = 'SALES';
```

This query, when executed against a remote database, will create a table called EMP and populate it across the network with the query's result set (see Figure 8.1).

The advantage of manual replication is that the databases are not continuously exchanging data. Setup and maintenance are easy, and errors are discovered during the move and can be corrected on the spot. Because

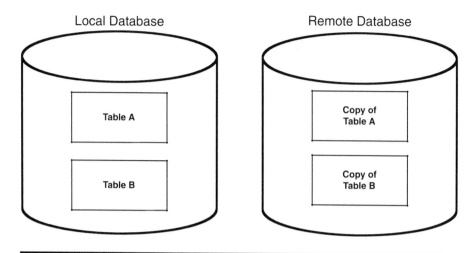

Figure 8.1   Replication of Table A and Table B.

the databases are not actively replicating changes, there is no additional replication load on either database.

The drawbacks of this type of replication are many. Because the databases are not propagating changes between them, the datasets will begin to drift apart, resulting in different answers depending on which database one queries. This may not be a problem if one system is used for reporting and users understand that the reports are as-of the refresh date. Another significant problem is that with large datasets, periodic refreshes can take a significant amount of time and bandwidth. Copying a 500-MB table across a network can take hours. Even if one uses a script only to move data that has changed, one is going to use a considerable amount of time and computer resources to update manually replicated data. Manual replication becomes even more complicated when both databases are being updated and it is completely inappropriate when the replication schema contains more than two databases.

Manual replication is most often used to periodically populate a reporting database or load data into a data warehouse. Because manual replication becomes unwieldy as the dataset gets larger, other methods of replicating data have been developed to automate some of the tasks.

STANDBY DATABASE

Another way to replicate data is to use a standby database. A standby database allows one to create an exact copy of the database and replicate changes on the primary database to the standby in real-time. For most enterprise database systems, implementing a standby database is fairly easy, but it is not as flexible as replication in many ways; it may or may not be the right solution for a particular situation. The advantage of a standby database is that changes to the primary database are automatically propagated to the standby database in real-time. The disadvantage is that the standby database normally cannot be used while in the standby mode. To generate reports, one would switch it from the standby mode to a read-only mode, generate the reports, and then switch it back to standby mode. This method provides the ability to periodically use the standby database for reporting and to have an operational backup database in the event of a failure of the primary database. The disadvantage of a standby database is that it cannot be used while in standby mode and can only be used in a read-only mode, unless it becomes the primary database. For this reason, most enterprise database suppliers do not require additional licenses for the standby database.

REPLICATION USING TRIGGERS

Database triggers can be used to facilitate replication. The DBA (database administrator) can create a trigger that captures a row modification on a table and forwards that change to a remote table. If both tables implement the trigger, changes are propagated back and forth, keeping both tables in sync. This is more difficult than it might first appear, because the procedures must ensure that the trigger does not forward an update being propagated from another database, and they must implement some sort of primary key collision resolution, which is discussed later in this chapter. Likewise, the trigger must fire after the data is changed or a constraint violation may cause the transaction to fail after it is forwarded to remote sites.

If one requires this kind of replication, do not reinvent the wheel. Instead, use the replication provided by the database system.

REPLICATION USING VIEWS

Normally, views are used within a database schema to simplify SQL commands. They are stored as an SQL statement and used to create a dataset that can then be queried from, like a virtual table. In many databases, one can create a view that is an actual table in the database that can pre-aggregate or pre-join data, rather than a SQL statement. In an Oracle database, these objects are called *materialized views*. Once created, an application can query the materialized view, saving the resources needed to aggregate or join the data. In its simplest form, the materialized view could be a complete copy of the original table. Another significant advantage of a materialized view is that the database will update

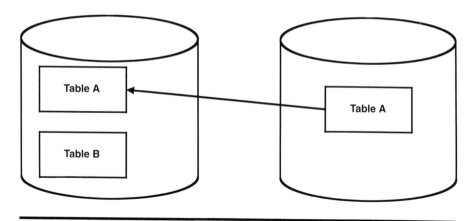

Figure 8.2 One-way replication.

the view as the data changes. When a row is inserted or changed, the view is updated within the parameters set when the materialized view was created. In this way, the materialized view remains up-to-date.

A materialized view is used to replicate data by building it into the remote database, or a base table in the primary database. The materialized view periodically checks the base table to update any changes.

ONE-WAY REPLICATION

One-way replication (see Figure 8.2) is the easiest replication scheme to design, implement, and maintain. The tables in the primary database function normally in a read-write mode, while the tables in the remote database are read-only. Inserts, updates, and deletes in a base table are propagated to the remote table. Because the remote table is read-only, all data integrity requirements reside in the primary database. This can be implemented manually using database triggers or using the database built-in replication capability, such as materialized views. One-way replication involves minimal database overhead and uses little network bandwidth because it only propagates changes in one direction. The disadvantage is that tables in the remote database are read-only.

WRITEABLE REPLICATION

Writeable replication is a form of one-way replication that allows remote databases to write to a replicated table. Only the changes made in the master database are replicated to the remote databases. Local changes in the remote databases are not replicated. This form of replication is used when implementing an application that must be able to update data to function, but only changes made at the master site need be replicated. For example, an application that maintains user data in a database table must be able to update that table to function or when the user logs off the data is removed. Implementing writeable replication on the tables, the application updates will allow them to stay current with the master database, while allowing the remote database to maintain the user data without propagating it to other databases in the scheme. One problem with using writeable replication is that if the table is not updated by row (i.e., a complete refresh), the local data may be removed by the refresh procedure. Like updateable or multi-master replication, steps must be taken to ensure that there are no primary key conflicts when using writeable replication.

UPDATEABLE REPLICATION

In updateable replication, both the primary and remote database tables can be updated simultaneously. This is referred to as updateable or multi-master replication. Updateable replication is much more difficult to design, create, and maintain because it introduces the problem of data collisions. For example, if a row is inserted into the remote table with the same primary key as a row in the base table, the row is not able to propagate because it will violate the primary key constraint; the base table will reject it. This can result in inconsistent datasets as rows are inserted into one table but rejected by the other.

The Push-Pull Method

One technique to implement updateable replication is called the push-pull method (see Figure 8.3). The remote site periodically pulls updates from the master site. When the remote site is updated, it will first push the change back to the master site and then pull all changes back from the master site. This can be implemented using either procedures or distributed transactions. For example, the remote database implements replication by pulling changes from the master site. When the remote application updates a row of data, this can be implemented as a distributed transaction against the master database, then forcing a refresh to bring the update back to the remote database. The advantage of using a distributed transaction for the data change is that referential integrity only needs to be implemented in the master database. If the data change violates referential integrity, the distributed transaction will fail, returning an error to the application. A disadvantage of using distributed queries is that it could induce a significant network delay to the transaction and the subsequent commit.

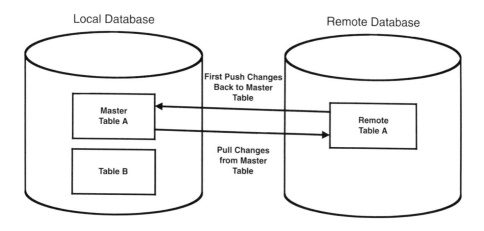

Figure 8.3   Push-Pull replication.

To resolve the delay inherent in distributed transactions, most modern databases implement some type of queue to handle the propagation of changes. The remote application will make a data change that is inserted into the remote table and queued to be sent to the master database. When the database refreshes the table, the queued changes are pushed to the master site, while all master site changes are pulled and applied to the remote table. This resolves the performance issues; however, it causes a number of other problems. First, referential integrity must now be maintained at all the remote sites. Second, some method must be implemented to resolve conflicts that arise during the data exchange. If the remote application inserts and commits a row of data that contains a key that will conflict with a key already in the master database table, the problem will arise when the remote site pushes the data to the master site. The master site will reject the row because of the key conflict. At this point, data has been committed in the remote database that cannot be replicated to the master database. The transaction cannot be rolled back because it had been committed in the remote database. Some type of conflict resolution must be implemented, as discussed later in this chapter.

The Multi-Master Method

In the push-pull method, there was only one master database to which all changes were first propagated. In the multi-master method (see Figure 8.4), each database acts as a master database, propagating to all other master databases in the scheme. Most enterprise-level databases have incorporated some type of multi-master replication into the database, which makes the setup and maintenance easier. Also, because it is built

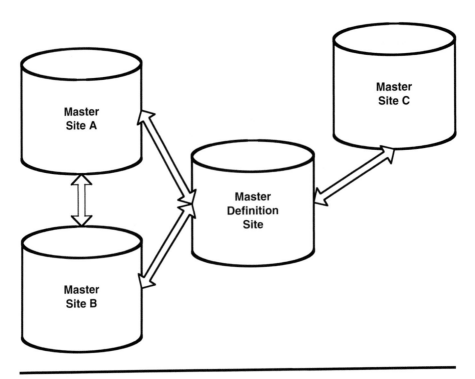

Figure 8.4 Multi-master replication.

into the database, multi-master replication can usually replicate additional database objects such as indexes, procedures, functions, and packages. Most implementations of multi-master replication use only a push.

Each site pushes committed changes to all other sites in the scheme. Each site must implement referential integrity and validate the incoming data. There are a number of downsides to multi-master replication, such as:

1. *Potentially large network bandwidth requirements.* Not only does multi-master replication push data to all other sites, but it must also send a significant amount of administrative data. For example, if two sites update the same row, the last one to commit the change overwrites the earlier change. This is also implemented in multi-master replication but it is more difficult because data is pushed at different times from each database.

2. *Reduced database performance.* Because multi-master replication involves a number of triggers, procedures, and queues, there is a lot of overhead within the database to maintain and propagate changes. This impact is significant enough to be noticed by users in a heavily loaded database.

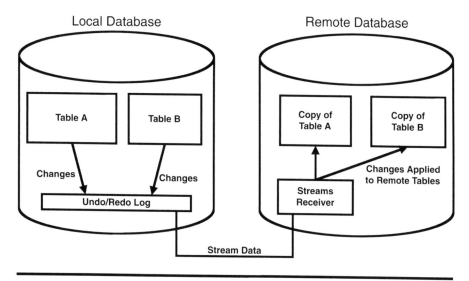

Figure 8.5 Streams replication.

3. *Increased administrative requirements.* Problem resolution becomes more difficult when replication is involved. When problems appear, the DBA must ensure that replication is not the cause and that the problem is not replicated to other sites. Database performance tuning and problem resolution become more complicated by an order of magnitude.
4. *Database changes require additional planning.* New versions of applications may require revisiting the replication design.

If the database in use implements multi-master replication, one may also have access to powerful features that allow one to make changes to database objects and propagate those changes to all other sites automatically.

The Streams Method

The final method of replication discussed here is relatively new and uses database change logs. It is referred to as *streams* because it reads the change logs, pulls out committed data changes, and sends them to the remote database (see Figure 8.5). The streams method can be built into the database one is using or can be implemented using a third-party application. By attaching a process that pulls committed changes from the change logs, streams replication is able to function without placing a significant load on the host database. When a committed change is found, it is sent to all other sites, where it is applied. Like multi-master replication, streams replication requires that each site implement referential integrity, including conflict resolution. Although streams replication reduces the load on the database, it comes with a price; streams replication has less capabilities and features than multi-master replication. To determine if streams replication meets specific needs, one must determine its capabilities in the database one is implementing.

WHAT ARE CONFLICTS?

The function of a primary key is to uniquely identify every row in the table. Inserting a row of data into a table with a primary key that is already in use will cause the insert to fail with a primary key conflict. This is how one differentiates the employees in the EMP table with the same name, like Robert Smith.

As discussed later in this chapter, most databases use the primary key to identify unique rows at all sites containing that table. But what if the tables do not contain a primary key? All tables in the replication environment contain a key that replication uses to uniquely identify rows across the separate master sites. When one creates a master site, all tables that do not have a primary key must have a column or columns identified that uniquely identify rows. Using these columns, one has, in fact, created a key for use in replication. Conflicts occur when data is propagated that conflicts with that key.

To greatly increase the efficiency of replication, most databases propagate transactions on a schedule. In updateable replication using a push-pull method, only the master site must ensure that the keys used for replication are not violated. When using a multi-master method of replication, each master site must verify replicated data before updating the local data. When a row is inserted into a table, the local key is checked and, if the data violates the key, the insert is refused. If the data does not violate the key, it is inserted into the table.

Key conflicts are just one conflict found in replication. When a receiver applies a transaction, it checks the before-image to ensure that the table data is still the same. What happens when one row of data is updated at two remote sites at the same time? The first update propagates normally and is applied; the second update follows and, because it expects the before-image to be the original data, it fails to be applied. The before-image is changed by the first update. This is called an update conflict. A delete conflict is similar: one site updates a row while another site deletes the row. If the update propagates first, the delete fails because the before-image does not match. If the delete propagates first, the row no longer exists when the update is applied. As one can see, getting a replication environment to function is just the beginning. To keep it operating, one needs to plan for conflict avoidance and create methods of conflict resolution.

Conflict avoidance is taking steps to ensure against conflicts arising. Conflict resolution is determining a method to automatically resolve conflicts. It is important that you plan for both. Proper planning will greatly reduce the number of conflicts generated by your replication scheme. However, once a conflict occurs, it must be dealt with quickly to ensure the integrity of later data changes. If a row is inserted in one database but refused by another because of a conflict, the two databases will begin to diverge. Future changes in that row can only occur on one of the replicated databases. Most databases will stop replicating and place all changes in a queue once an unresolved conflict occurs. Once the conflict is resolved, the queued changes can be applied and replication can continue. However, this manual method of resolution is costly — not only to the DBA, who must research and resolve the problem, but also to the company that may not have access to the database or worse, may get inconsistent data until the conflict is resolved.

Conflict Avoidance

Data conflicts arise due to referential integrity constraints, namely keys. Primary keys are used to uniquely identify a row in a table. Older replication methods could use table row IDs but that is discouraged because there is no real relationship between a row of data and its table row ID. A primary key, however, will uniquely identify a row in the table, independent of where in the table it is stored. Later in this chapter we discuss designing schema for replication. Each table will require a primary key. Even tables that allow redundant rows of data will need a primary key for each row. How does each database in a replication schema produce a unique primary key when it inserts a row? One can choose from a number of ways, depending on one's requirements.

1. *Central repository.* One database could be designated to generate primary keys for all other databases in the replication schema. A function could be created that, when called, would generate a primary key using a sequence that is unique. When a new row is inserted into a table, the database would make a remote call to the function to get a unique primary key value. To improve performance, the database may obtain keys in groups and store them in a local table for immediate use. The primary problem with this technique is that it depends on the designated database to generate the keys. If the database is down or the network connection is lost,

the local transaction would fail because it would not be able to obtain a new key.

2. *Assigning blocks of numbers.* If each database created its own primary keys from sequences, one could ensure uniqueness by assigning blocks of numbers to each database. This is accomplished by setting the sequence at each site to start at a different number. Site A would be assigned a sequence starting at 1 and ending at 99999999, Site B starts at 100000000 and ends at 199999999, Site C 200000000 to 299999999, etc. With a maximum value of 1.0E28, one has plenty of numbers to divide among the sites. The primary drawback to this approach is that it does not scale well when adding additional sites. If one divides the available numbers equally between all the sites, adding one site cuts the available numbers for one site in half to make room for the new site.

3. *Assign a site prefix.* A more flexible and scalable approach is to have all sites start their sequence at 1 and add a site prefix to the sequence number. Normally, the prefix is the database name so that one can see which database added the row. If "my database" is called MYDB, the first three rows would be mydb1, mydb2, and mydb3. Because each database should have a unique name, keys generated by the database will not clash with or affect keys generated by other sites.

As one can see, conflict avoidance must be part of replication planning. However, no matter how diligent one is with conflict avoidance, one will eventually have a conflict that needs to be resolved.

Database Conflict Resolution

Establishing conflict resolution is a process of defining rules for the database to apply when a conflict is detected. If the conflict is resolved, the transaction does not end up in the error queue and replication continues. One establishes conflict resolution on groups of columns in a table and defines a priority for each type of resolution. Conflict resolution does not have to be defined only on keys; however, it is a key conflict that triggers the conflict resolution. The following list details different conflict resolution methods that Oracle database makes available:

1. *Latest timestamp.* When a transaction fails because the before-image has changed, the column timestamps of the transactions are compared; and if the second transaction is later than the one changing the before-image, the second transaction is applied and overlays

the current data (which contains the first transaction). To implement *latest timestamp*, one must include a Date column in the table and use a trigger to load the server date/time upon insert. This method closely mimics how a local database functions; whoever commits last, wins. One can also implement an *earliest timestamp* method.

2. *Minimum/maximum value.* When a column has a conflict between two transactions, the minimum value method is triggered, which evaluates the current and new values of a defined column and selects the lower value (or higher for maximum) to determine if the new column is applied.

3. *Group priority value.* In this case, column groups are assigned a priority and conflicts are adjudicated to the highest priority group.

4. *Site priority value.* In this instance, sites are assigned a priority. When two transactions conflict, the transaction from the master site with the highest priority will be applied. This is actually a special case of the *group priority value* method above.

One can define multiple resolution methods on a single table and the database will attempt to execute them to resolve the conflict. For example, one could implement the *latest timestamp* method, followed by *site priority*, on the EMP table. When the database encounters a conflict on the EMP table, it would attempt to use the latest timestamp first; if that fails, it would use site priority. If all defined conflict resolution methods are unable to resolve the conflict, the database will place the transaction in the error queue for manual resolution. Remember that conflict resolution can never perform a rollback of the transaction because the transaction has been successfully committed on at least one site.

WHICH FORM OF REPLICATION IS RIGHT FOR YOU?

Determining which type of replication a situation requires is very important. Remember these two adages:

1. More is NOT always better!
2. Just because a database includes it, you do NOT have to use it!

One of the biggest mistakes a company can make is to implement multi-master replication when it only needs one-way views. With replication, "more" is harder to implement, harder to maintain, harder to troubleshoot, and takes more time.

Here are some criteria that one can use to determine the level of replication that best fits a specific situation.

1. *Is the transfer of data time sensitive?* Many DBAs believe that data is time sensitive when, in fact, it is not. If the data is being moved to a data warehouse to be used for data mining, or report generation, the data probably is not time sensitive. A daily or even weekly transfer may meet the entire business requirement. Ask management if a daily report in the morning is acceptable, instead of a report available on demand with the most recent data. Many DBAs are finding that even internal materialized views are taking so long to update that they have to update them at night or only on weekends.

2. *Is the number of tables manageable?* If using an ERP application with thousands of tables and indexes, forget about replicating the entire database. This is not a candidate for replication. However, replicating parts of large databases is possible. Remember that each replicated object adds overhead to the databases and takes network bandwidth. There are practical limits to the number of objects that one can replicate, depending on the capability of the database server and the network connections. Replicating a hundred tables is easy; a thousand may not be possible; ten thousand — forget it.

3. *Do all your replicated tables need to be updateable?* This is important. A shop will often set up full multi-master replication because the database is supporting an application that must update certain tables. Tables that need updating at both locations must use updateable replication; however, all remaining tables can use one-way replication. This ability to mix replication types can significantly lower the replication overhead. Remember: less is best.

4. *Does your database change constantly?* Does QA roll in a new update every weekend? If so, replication may not be for you. Table changes may force one either to rebuild the replication or implement multi-master replication. Maintaining replication in a changing database will entail a significant increase in the DBA's workload.

5. *Is the number of transactions manageable?* The number of transactions per minute is another variable that must be considered. A replication based on a few tables will be better able to handle high numbers of transactions. A large replication may not be able to keep up on a high transaction system; this again depends on the server capabilities and the network bandwidth.

6. *Are you replicating between different versions of a database or different operating systems?* Many shops choose replication precisely because replication can operate between either different versions of the database, or between databases running on different operating systems. Because replication is passed across network links, different versions of the database can be used. There are a number of third-party solutions that will allow one to replicate between databases of different manufacturers.

7. *Do both sites require the ability to update the same tables?* If both sides of the replication must update data (insert, update, delete), then one must implement advanced replication. Use updateable replication only on the tables that must be updated on both sides of the replication.
8. *Does the replicated site require the ability to replicate to another site?* A master site can replicate with other sites. If the remote site only replicates with one master site, use updateable views. If the remote site must replicate the data further, then it too must be a master site and multi-master replication is required.

As one might have figured, replication is difficult to understand and time-consuming to set up. However, its daunting reputation is much worse than reality. Once it is set up and operating, one will find that it really is not very intimidating. Remember to replicate at the lowest level possible. Do not try to replicate more objects than the server and network are able to support.

PLANNING YOUR REPLICATION SCHEMA

Primary Keys

Having determined the replication requirements, one must ensure that the schema is ready for replication. The first requirement for all tables that will be replicated is that they contain a primary key. Some database systems will allow one to define columns to be used to uniquely identify rows; however, this is not recommended. When one uses columns to define uniqueness within replication, one has — in essence — defined a key only for replication. This can lead to confusion when local systems can insert data that the replication system cannot propagate. We recommend that you always define primary keys in the schema to avoid confusion.

Foreign Keys

Foreign keys pose a special problem because the child/parent table may not be part of the replication schema. If the child table is replicated without the parent table, the foreign key cannot be enforced. To ensure that the foreign key constraint is not violated, both tables must be in the replication schema. However, most DBAs place an index on the foreign key column of the parent table to remove the full table scan required on the parent table when the child table is updated. If the database system will support replicating the foreign key index, the constraint can be maintained at the remote sites, even when the parent table is not part of the replication.

Indexes

Other than foreign key indexes, indexes are not normally replicated. Indexes would be built locally on the replicated tables. This ensures that they are maintained locally and are valid against the supported table.

Denormalization

When evaluating replication requirements, one can gain some performance increase by replicating pre-joined tables. By pre-joining tables in the replication schema, the overhead of the join happens during propagation rather than during queries. This can result in a significant performance increase if the remote database is used for aggregating data for reports or data warehousing.

Moving Large Datasets

Normally, replication moves data one row or change at a time. If one inserts a hundred rows at one site, they are inserted one row at a time at the remote sites. The actual propagation across the network may happen in groups but the application of the change is one at a time, in order. If one is planning on replicating a large table with millions of rows, the physical movement of the data across the network and the application at the remote site could take hours or days. Normally, when a database is propagating data, both the local and remote site tables will be read-only until the propagation is completed. This means that during the time it takes to establish a replication scheme, neither database will be available for normal use. This is a significant problem if it takes multiple days to instantiate the remote site. Most database systems allow one to move the data to the remote site before creating replication. This is known as *offline instantiation*.

Offline instantiation allows one to move the data to the remote site and then build the replication around the data already located there. However, it is not as easy as it appears. First, the base objects (tables, indexes, etc.) must be read-only from the time the data begins moving until the replication is established. If the base objects are updated, the replicated copy will start out of synch. For a large database, the time it takes to export data, transmit it across the network, and import it into the remote database can still take days. Once the data is in the remote database, one essentially builds the replication on top of the current tables.

Loading data can also pose a problem. If one uses a bulk method to load large amounts of data into the local database, it may take hours for the rows to propagate to the remote sites. This overhead on the databases and the network may be acceptable. If not, one will need to be prepared to load the data at each remote site. The database system will have a method to temporarily turn off replication. Once off, the data can be loaded without the changes propagating to other sites. When the load is completed, turn back on the replication and new changes will begin propagating. Two notes of caution when using this method: (1) the databases will be out of synch until the data load is completed at each site; and (2) any changes made while the replication is turned off will not propagate and will result in data divergence between sites.

Resynching Data

Most databases that support multi-master replication will have a utility to locate and re-synch data among the separate replication sites. Most of these utilities are rather primitive and must be used with caution. If the problem was caused by updates while replication was off, updates will cause conflicts because the before-image is not correct. Having implemented conflict resolution using the latest timestamp method will allow the database to correct the problem automatically as the data continues to be updated. Using one of the re-synching utilities normally involves picking one site as correct and then re-synching each remote site with that site. It is a two-step process: (1) delete rows that do not match the correct site, and then (2) add all the rows missing to the remote site. Because this is a row-by-row analysis, using a re-synching utility can take a considerable amount of time.

SUMMARY

Replication is an advanced database feature that takes careful planning and preparation to execute. Each enterprise database system has its own unique method for implementing and monitoring database replication. Each level of replication has its advantages and disadvantages, and it is important to understand your needs before beginning replication planning. Implement replication at the lowest level possible to meet your needs.

Only replicate the database objects needed at the remote sites. Do not replicate indexes, except to support a foreign key when the parent table is not replicated. Plan your methodology for moving large datasets to remote sites.

Finally, plan and implement for conflict avoidance, but always implement conflict resolution when running any type of updateable replication.

9

DESIGN OF THE
OLTP DATABASE

DESIGNING FOR ONLINE TRANSACTION PROCESSING

Most texts on database design focus on OLTP (online transaction processing) design in general and have a section that focuses on data warehouse design. This chapter discusses specific areas required for effective OLTP design and Chapter 9 introduces design criteria for the data warehouse.

Online transaction processing (OLTP) usually means executing a very large number of small transactions very quickly. In many cases, there is a user waiting for the operation to complete before executing the next action. Speed is very important. Users have become accustomed to applications that respond immediately and will no longer tolerate slow performance. The Internet has placed another demand of application performance because a company Web site may be the only customer interaction a company has. A slow-performing Web site will negatively impact customer satisfaction. Another problem is that the company may have thousands of customers using the Web site at the same time. The design of the database used to support transaction-processing applications must reflect this need to execute quickly and efficiently.

The term "transaction" has special meaning in the database world. A transaction is a group of database operations that are related and must be committed or rolled back as a single unit. In this chapter, we refer to individual database queries (i.e., selects, updates, inserts, and deletes) as operations and transactions will retain the traditional meaning of groups of operations.

Because OLTP transactions normally involve small amounts of data, the database must be designed and implemented to support efficient caching of SQL and data. Unlike in a data warehouse environment, OLTP systems tend to execute the same SQL with different values that retrieve specific information.

NORMALIZATION

Because OLTP systems tend to access individual pieces of data, there are advantages to fully normalizing database schema. Normalization was discussed in detail in Chapter 4; refer to that chapter for additional information about normalization techniques. For most applications, third normal form (3NF) provides a good trade-off between performance and data availability; however, the higher normal forms (BCNF, 4NF, and 5NF) may provide additional performance benefits based on how the application accesses the data. In discussing normalization, we exclude the issue of data storage space requirements because that is rarely an issue with modern database management systems; here, we are strictly basing the design on database transaction execution. Placing the schema in 3NF or higher provides the ability to atomically access a piece of data while limiting the amount of unneeded information that must be included in the access. Because all modern enterprise database management systems access data in fixed-size chunks (some systems call this a page or a block), normalizing the schema will allow the block to contain more of the requested data and less extraneous data. The downside of over-normalizing schema is that the database will have to join tables to retrieve the information it needs. Joining tables is an additional step that reduces performance. So, the focus of normalizing the schema is to allow the retrieval of specific data without forcing joins or including unneeded data in the block requested. Another normalization issue is maintaining the integrity of the data. By normalizing the data so that each piece of information is stored in one location, updates and inserts need only change or insert new data in one location. Redundant data within the schema will slow updates and inserts because the data must be implemented in multiple locations to ensure data integrity, thus significantly slowing execution.

Denormalization is taking a normalized database and adding back some data redundancy to improve performance. Although this is very common in data warehousing, it should be performed with care when implemented in an OLTP design. An example of denormalization would be creating a table containing the sum of each product sold by day. This table can be used to significantly improve generating reports that require this data. However, once created, the data for the current day quickly becomes inaccurate as additional orders are added into the system. If the table is to remain current, it must be updated after each new or changed order is committed. The overhead of maintaining the redundant data can quickly exceed the advantage it provides. Denormalization is usually found

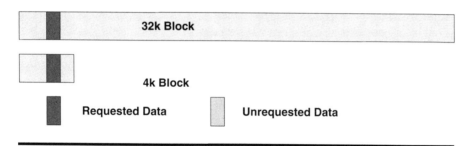

Figure 9.1 Large and small blocks.

in databases that support both OLTP and reporting/decision support systems. Without the redundancy, the reporting system is too slow to use; adding the redundancy will slow down the OLTP operations and cause customer complaints. The designer must work with management to implement a solution that will satisfy the reporting/DSS needs while not impacting the OLTP operation. One common method involves adding tables with aggregate data that is refreshed at a specified interval, rather than with each commit, and ensuring that everyone who uses the reports understands that the data is as of the last refresh. In this case, the tables supporting the reporting/DSS application are like a schema within the OLTP schema, and many implementations actually move the reporting data to their own schema, although this greatly reduces the flexibility of the reporting schema to adapt to changing requirements.

Whether operating a strictly OLTP system or a hybrid OLTP/reporting system, one must normalize the data to allow efficient access to the individual data elements used by the application.

DATA STORAGE

Data storage applies to two separate areas: (1) the data block that the information is stored on and (2) how the data is stored on the physical disk. The data block or page determines how much data is read or written with each I/O. Because the database will access the data by reading a block, a larger block will return more data (see Figure 9.1). As discussed in the previous section, normalizing the data will ensure that the data returned in the block is relevant to the request. The optimal size of the data block is defined by how the application queries the data. If the application constantly retrieves ranges of data — order records from the last seven days, for instance — it will need to read multiple blocks to obtain the information it needs and larger blocks could improve the performance. On the other hand, most OLTP systems access specific information such as the order_date for order number 204957. If that piece of information is stored on a large block, the I/O will return not only the requested data, but also all the other data on the block that is not needed.

When it comes to the physical I/O to retrieve the block from disk, the advantage of small blocks is negated by the operating systems method of reading the hard drive. An operating system that reads 32k segments for each read will be able to read a 32k data block as efficiently as it can read a 4k block; the size of the data block impacts the OS I/O as it exceeds the size of the OS read block. However, the size of the data block has a significant impact on the efficiency of the database data cache.

Database Data Cache Efficiency

All enterprise-level databases management systems implement some type of cache to hold frequently used data in memory. This reduces database response time because the database has direct access to the data rather than having to first retrieve it from disk using a physical I/O. The efficiency of the data cache is paramount to the database's performance. Theoretically, if there were enough memory to cache all the data in the database, one would eliminate the physical I/O problem completely. In reality, with today's terabyte databases, this goal is unachievable. Because we cannot cache the entire dataset, it is important to cache only the most requested data. The database management system will implement some form of a "most recently used" algorithm to keep frequently accessed blocks in the data cache. How we store our data on a block can improve or hinder the efficiency of this cache.

An OLTP application normally accesses small amounts of data at a time. If we implement the database using a large block to hold data, there will be a large amount of unrequested data surrounding the data requested. The unrequested data is stored in the data cache along with the requested data. The larger the block, the more unrequested data will enter the cache. For example, if one uses 32k blocks and the data cache can only hold ten blocks, the first ten requests will fill the data cache, assuming the data requested was on ten separate blocks. For this example, each request is for data not in the cache. After ten requests, the data cache will look something like Figure 9.2.

Assuming each piece of data is equal in size and the requested data is 320 bytes, each block holds 100 separate pieces of data and the cache's space efficiency is about 1 percent. Each new request for data not in the cache will result in replacing 10 percent of the cache.

If one used 8k blocks instead of 32k blocks, the cache efficiency would increase substantially. The cache will not hold 40 blocks in the same memory space. So, one would need 40 requests for data not in the data cache before one has to age out a block. Figure 9.3 shows the improvement in cache efficiency.

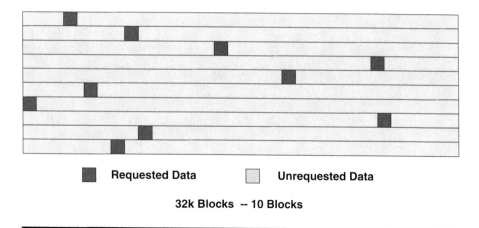

Figure 9.2 Data cache with large blocks.

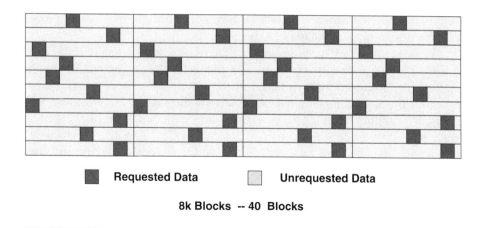

Figure 9.3 Data cache with medium blocks.

You now have a more efficient data cache utilizing 4 percent of the cache space with requested data. Each block only holds 25 pieces of data so that space efficiency goes up to 4 percent. There is four times as much requested data in the data cache.

If one now changes to 2k blocks, the data cache will hold 160 blocks, resulting in a space efficiency of one requested piece of data to five unrequested pieces of data, or 16 percent of the cache will have requested data. The data cache now looks like Figure 9.4.

Remember that we are using an application that is working on a small individual piece of data and comparing only cache space use (requested data versus unrequested data). Due to the varying size of data, there is

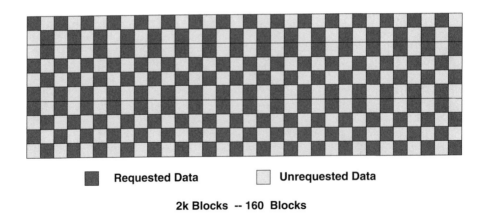

Requested Data   **Unrequested Data**

2k Blocks -- 160 Blocks

Figure 9.4 Data cache with small blocks.

no way to get perfect space efficiency and, as with all design decisions, setting the block size is a trade-off between efficient access of small pieces of data and range/full scans of tables.

While small block sizes provide efficient access of specific data, they have a performance impact on queries that scan data to extract ranges or aggregates (sums, count, avg., etc.). If the query must execute a full table scan, all the table blocks must be read into the cache. Small blocks will result in a higher number of I/Os than larger blocks. One of the fastest ways to improve query performance is to add indexes so that the database can locate specific data by searching an index before retrieving the row from the table. Because indexes contain a small amount of ordered data — normally one to three table columns — that is scanned for values, they perform better when placed on large data blocks. Each large block will contain more of the index, so fewer blocks need to be scanned to locate specific data. Because all databases will perform both scans and individual data reads, the designer must select a block size that will improve the overall database performance.

Some database management systems, like Oracle, provide the capability to create a database with multiple block sizes. The different-sized blocks are placed in separate caches designated for that block size. This will allow the designer to place data on small blocks and indexes on larger blocks. Using multiple block sizes complicates the design but can provide performance benefits, if implemented correctly.

Data Growth

When designing the database to support OLTP applications, one must understand how the applications inserts and updates data. In normal OLTP

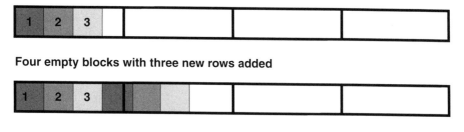

Four empty blocks with three new rows added

Rows 1,2,3 are updated, causing all three to chain to a new block

Rows 1,2,3 are updated again, causing all to chain to more than two blocks

Figure 9.5   Chained rows.

operations, new records are inserted with incomplete data and then updated when the remaining data is obtained. For example, when a clerk selects the *new order* button, the application inserts a new order record in the order table with the date and order number; all other fields are blank. When the clerk fills out the order form and submits the order, the application updates the order record with the additional information. As the order is filled, the application records dates and events until the order has been delivered to the customer and the order is marked completed. When we look at the life of the database row that contains the data about this order, we see that when initially inserted in the order table, it was very small, containing only the date and the order number. Let us assume it was 100 bytes of data. Once the order entry was completed, the row was updated and with the additional information grew to 500 bytes. By the time the order is completed and closed out, the record may be 1k. An 8k block will hold approximately eight completed orders. The problem arises because this row is growing over time and the database does not know how large the row will grow. If you have 100 clerks entering new orders, one block could get 30 new orders inserted. Each of these order rows will then grow as additional order information is added or updated; eventually, the data will fill the block and the row will expand to another block. This is referred to as a chained row and is depicted in Figure 9.5.

Chained rows cause the database to read two blocks to get one row and can have a significant impact on query performance. Even if both blocks are in the data cache, there are still multiple reads for each row. In a high transaction load OLTP system, it is not uncommon for rows to

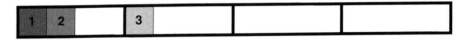

Four empty blocks with three new rows added

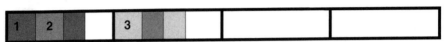

Rows 1,2,3 are updated, causing only one row to chain to a new block

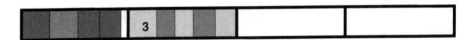

Rows 1,2,3 are updated again, causing only one chained row

Figure 9.6   Using PCTFREE to stop chained rows.

chain to three or four blocks, although they are only a small portion of the size of a block. To fix a table with chained rows, the DBA will need to rebuild the table. However, if no action is taken to resolve the problem, the database will simply begin chaining rows in the rebuilt table.

To stop the database from creating chained rows, the database designer must implement a way for the database to retain space in the blocks for row expansion. This can greatly reduce and possibly stop row chaining. In an Oracle database, each table has a storage parameter called PCTFREE that defines a percentage of the block saved for row expansion (see Figure 9.6). In SQL Server, chained rows are called page splitting and the parameter fill factor is used to ensure that space is available for row expansion.

Finally, reserving space for row expansion limits the amount of data that can be on each block or page. The trade-off is possible unused space on the block against chained rows. For this reason, the PCTFREE/fillfactor is set for each table in the database. Tables that do not experience row expansion should be set to utilize most of the block, while tables with row expansion should reserve enough space to prevent chained rows.

SQL REUSE

Online transactions processing applications tend to execute the same queries over and over again. Each time a database receives a new SQL statement, it must be parsed, verified, and checked to ensure that the user has access to the requested data. Next, the database creates an execution plan that it uses to retrieve the data and satisfy the query. The creation of the execution plan is a time-consuming and costly operation for the database management system. Many times, the time spent creating the execution plan exceeds the time it takes to execute the execution plan and retrieve the data. For this reason, modern database management systems implement an SQL cache where frequently executed SQLs are stored along with the execution plan. In a well-tuned database, all the SQLs will eventually be stored in the SQL cache and will execute using already-calculated execution plans. However, the application must be designed to take advantage of this capability through the use of bind variables. In the example below, the query returns an employee record for employee number 10422:

```
SELECT *
FROM EMP
WHERE EMP_NUMBER = 10422;
```

In the query, the employee number is a literal. Each time the application executes this query with a different employee number, the database sees the query as a new SQL and must create a new execution plan. However, if you replace the literal with a variable, the database will see each of these queries as the same SQL, get the execution plan from the SQL cache, substitute the value of the variable, and retrieve the information.

```
SELECT *
FROM EMP
WHERE EMP_NUMBER = :var_emp_num;
```

All modern languages support the use of bind variables within the database access library. In Java, bind variables are implemented using prepared statements:

```
//  con is the connection object
query1 = con.prepareStatement(
          "select * from emp where emp_number = ?");

query1.setInt(1,10422);
ResultSet rs = query1.execute();
```

In the example above, we already have our connection object called "con." We use the connection object to create a prepared statement called query1. Now, throughout the application, when we need an employee's data, we can use query1. The question mark in the prepared statement is where the variables are substituted. A prepared statement can have multiple variables, each defined by a question mark. If we want the employee data for employee number 10422, we define the variable by calling the setInt method of the prepared statement, passing it a 1 (substitute for the first variable in the prepared statement) and the employee number. If the prepared statement contained more variables, we would set each one in a similar fashion. Once the variables are set, we execute the query by calling the execute method and return the results to the ResultSet named "rs." When the execute method is called, the JDBC library passes the SQL to the database along with the variables. The database will look for the query in the SQL cache and, if it finds it, will take the execution plan, substitute the variables, retrieve the requested data, and return it to the JDBC connection. The application can reuse the prepared statement over and over again by setting the variable to the employee number needed and calling the execute method. The database will only create an execution plan the first time the query is executed; after that, it will reuse the execution plan stored in the SQL cache.

DATABASE LOCKING AND WAITING

Earlier, we discussed the data cache and SQL cache and how they can be used to improve transaction performance. At one time, DBAs focused their tuning efforts on achieving good cache hit ratios. While the cache-hit ratio is important, modern database management systems have highly optimized cache control algorithms. However, a perfectly optimized cache will not improve transactional performance on queries that are waiting behind locks. Because OLTP databases have multiple transactions occurring simultaneously, locks are used to serialize access to objects that can only support one operation at a time. Each database vendor has proprietary methods of implementing locks, so there is not an over-encompassing method to reduce them. Some database management systems implement row-level locking while others implement block-level locking. If we update a row in a table, transactions are blocked from that row during the update. Once the update is completed, the row is again available for use. If the database vendor implements block- or page-level locking, an update to a row will lock all the rows contained in that block or page, potentially causing additional processes to wait, even if they are not accessing the row that is being updated.

Some database vendors will lock a row, block, or page after an update until the update is committed or rolled back. This can cause a significant amount of blocking and waiting in a highly loaded OLTP system. The Oracle database implements a consistent view to get around locking a row until a commit is issued. When a row is updated, it is locked only during the update. After the update, the row is unlocked but other transactions will not see the update until the updating process commits the change. Until the commit is issued, other transactions will see the row data as it was before the update. In this way, the time between updates and commits will not affect the performance of other transactions.

A wait is caused by a process being blocked while attempting to access some object. Normally, waits are very short but the many concurrent transactions executing at the same time can cause waits to add up to a noticeable delay. Enterprise database management systems implement a wait interface that will allow one to determine what objects the transactions are waiting on. It is important to monitor locking and waiting and take action to reduce their impact on database transactions.

DEADLOCKS

A deadlock occurs when two transactions are waiting on a lock held by the other transaction. Neither will release its lock until it gets the other lock. The result is that the two transactions will sit, each waiting for the other. Of course, all other transactions needing those locks will back up behind them, sometimes bringing the database to a halt. Some database management systems will detect a deadlock and roll back one transaction, allowing the other to continue. If the system does not fix deadlocks automatically, it is up to the DBA to kill one process to break the deadlock. Deadlocks can negatively impact all the transactions running on a database. The level of row or page locking can affect how often a deadlock occurs; however, for the most part, a deadlock is an application design problem, not a database problem. If your system is having deadlock problems, you must analyze what objects are causing the deadlock and why the transaction is obtaining one lock and not releasing it before obtaining the other lock.

ROLLBACKS

Database management systems assume that changed data will be committed and as such will optimize the transaction toward a commit. When a rollback is encountered, it is an expensive operation to perform, both in terms of I/O and CPU time. If an application is performing an excessive amount of transaction rollbacks, one will need to determine the cause. Sometimes, it may require user training, but it is normally the result of poor application design. What are excessive rollbacks? If more than 0.1 percent of transactions roll back, you have a rollback problem in an OLTP database. For example, if 1.0 percent of transactions roll back and you normally have 100 concurrent transactions executing in the database, one transaction will always be rolling back. The goal is for rollbacks to be very rare.

INDEXING

Indexing an OLTP database is an important part of the database design. Indexes are the easiest way to improve the performance of long-running queries caused by full table scans. Too many indexes will also slow down the performance of updates and inserts. Too few indexes and all types of queries may run slower, even updates and deletes. If it were just a trade-off — performance of updates and inserts versus performance of selects — optimizing indexes in a database would be fairly easy. However, it is not that simple. The first is: is the index being used? If it is used, is it the correct index? Is there a better index? If the database is slow because of too many indexes, what method can one use to determine which indexes to remove?

Finding and removing indexes that are not used will improve database performance by removing the maintenance overhead. However, finding and removing duplicate indexes can have just as great an effect, if not more. The plan of attack is to locate all indexes that the database is currently not using. These unused indexes can then be removed from the database. Next, locate possible duplicate indexes. Duplicate indexes can be removed or modified to meet the requirements of the SQL statements. In reviewing index optimization, one may find tables that should be rebuilt as *index organized tables* or specialty indexes that might improve performance; this depends on the capabilities and features of the database one is using. Remember that OLTP systems perform lots of small updates and inserts. Too many indexes will begin to adversely affect query performance.

The first step is to locate unused indexes. Just because one adds an index does not mean that the database will use it in the execution plans. Modern databases will evaluate how effective it believes an index is before implementing it. Many unused indexes are the result of adding another index. The database was using index A but when index B was added, the database determined that B was a better index and no longer used index A. The ease with which one can locate unused indexes varies between database vendor and even database version. If the database management system one is using has the ability to track index use, one can use it to determine which indexes are not being used. Be sure to monitor the database through normal operation and include reporting periods, such as weekly or monthly reports.

If the database does not have a feature to monitor index use, one will have to manually determine which indexes are used. This will involve running each query, procedure, and function and examining the execution plan used by the database. This is a time-consuming and difficult task that must be repeated periodically. If possible, a script should be created that will gather execution plans from the SQL cache. This will provide a list of used indexes, from which one can derive the list of unused indexes.

Once one has a list of indexes that have not been used, we recommend using a tool or script and punching out the DDL required to rebuild them before dropping them. Also, watch for foreign key (FK) indexes. Some databases will not list the access of an index used to verify a foreign key. Removing FK indexes can cause large numbers of full table scans during inserts and updates. Now one can start dropping indexes and monitoring the system for increased response time or increases in full table scans.

Many of the systems that support a custom application are over-indexed. Once the unused indexes are removed, overall database performance should improve. If not, one may need to remove some indexes that are being used but that can be satisfied using another index. We refer to a duplicate index as two indexes that can both be used by a query and provide acceptable performance. Finding duplicate indexes is more of an art than a hard and fast rule. Our methodology is to go table-by-table, analyzing the indexes against the SQL to identify indexes that can be removed or should be changed. The goal in index optimization is to use only enough indexes to reach performance requirements. More is not better! It is relatively easy to identify possible duplicates; it is much more difficult to figure out which duplicate indexes to remove or modify. Below are some scenarios where one might be able to remove duplicate indexes.

Primary Keys

Any table with a PK (primary key) has an index on that PK. If one does not specify a PK index, the system will create one itself. It is very common to find redundant indexes based on the assumption that there is no index on the table's PK, when in fact there always is.

Table with Three or More Columns

Index1	column1_PK	
Index2	column1	column2
Index3	column1	column2column3

In this case, Index2 is redundant because it is completely contained in Index3. If Index1 were not a primary key index, it could possibly be redundant.

Multiple Indexes with the Most Restrictive Lead Columns

Index1	column1_PK	
Index2	column2	
Index3	column1	column2 ...
Index4	column2	column1 ...

In this case, Index3 and Index4 were created to support queries that contained both column1 and column2 in separate WHERE clauses. These indexes were added because in some queries column1 is more restrictive, it is the lead column; in other queries, column2 is more restrictive and, thus, the lead column. In fact, either Index3 or Index4 will satisfy the queries and will have equivalent performance. Having the lead column as the most restrictive column will not affect the index performance. In this case, one can drop either Index3 or Index4 and not affect query performance.

Large Multi-Column Indexes

Multi-column indexes with more than three columns may not provide more efficient access than a two- or three-column index. The objective of the index is to reduce the amount of rows returned from a table access. Therefore, to be effective, each added column must substantially reduce the number of returned rows. For example, assuming a large table, on a query with five or more WHERE (AND) clauses using a five-column index may return only one row. However, using a three-column index may return only 50 rows. A two-column index returns 200 rows. The time it takes to extract the one row from the 200 rows using nested-loops is negligible. Thus, the two-column index may be almost as efficient or fast as the five-column index. The key is to index the most restrictive columns. Another trade-off is a table with multiple column indexes where the leading column(s) are the same. For example, a table with four three-column indexes, where the leading two columns are the same, may work very efficiently on select statements but cause a heavy penalty on inserts and updates. Just one two-column index on the leading two columns may provide acceptable query performance while greatly improving inserts, updates, and deletes.

Organizing Tables as Indexes

Finally, small tables with two or three columns may benefit by being rebuilt as an *index organized table* (IOT). A two-column table with a PK and a two-column index has 1.5 times the data in indexes that are in the table. Making the table an IOT reduced the need for indexes because the table is the index. Also, IOTs can have indexes on non-leading columns, if required. Again, this must be balanced with the overhead of maintaining the IOT. Not all databases support IOTs.

Index efficiency is difficult. Many times, finding the best index is a matter of trial and error. Removing unused indexes is the easy part. Finding the most efficient index for a system is more of an art. Always remember that changing an index can have a cascading effect on many SQL statements' execution plans. Once one removes the unused and redundant indexes, one must continue to monitor performance because query execution plans will change as the database grows.

SUMMARY

OLTP databases are designed to handle large numbers of concurrent, small transactions. Because OLTP systems access small amounts of data, they must be designed to optimize database storage structures and caches. Once the database is in operation, one must monitor performance to ensure that the database remains optimized as the data grows. The appearance of chained rows indicates improper storage parameters that may require that the table be rebuilt. Focus on reducing waiting and locking, removing all rollbacks, and ensuring that the database is indexed for optimal performance.

10

DESIGN OF DATA WAREHOUSES AND DECISION SUPPORT SYSTEM DATABASES

WHAT IS A DATA WAREHOUSE?

A data warehouse is a database used to store integrated information gathered from separate and sometimes diverse sources. Normally, the data is gathered and staged in a location where it can be integrated into the data warehouse schema.

Because the data originates from separate systems, such as point-of-sales systems or office/branch databases, the data must be transformed to integrate into the warehouse scheme and to integrate with data already in the warehouse. For example, a large company may have multiple departments that need information about a product. The Denver office may need a product and orders it through the company's point-of-sales (POS) system. The POS will check the local inventory and send the part, if in stock; otherwise, it will send the request to the product warehouse. This separate system will check the local inventory and either ship or order the product. The company's shipping department will track the product pickup and delivery times. To improve operations, the company wants to know how often the product is available versus ordered from the local inventory and the warehouse. They also want to track how long it takes to ship the product from each level and the average amount of time that each office waits to receive requested products. This simple example appears easy to calculate. Now, what if there are hundreds or thousands of products, 200 local offices with local inventories, and you want the average to be by month for the past two years? Add to the problem that each department implements different database schemas/programs to maintain the data and one sees that the information quickly becomes too great to handle without some type of automation, such as a data warehouse.

Using a data warehouse, the company will periodically gather the data from each of the separate systems into a staging location. Here, the data is transformed into a usable form; for example, the inventory data is linked with the shipping data so that an order can be tracked as it moves forward through the system. Once the data has been transformed and possibly aggregated, it is moved from the staging location into the data warehouse.

Once in the data warehouse, knowledge tools, data mining, and decision support programs analyze the data and help the company make decisions, such as what quantity of a product should be maintained in inventory at each level to reduce storage costs while improving customer support.

OLAP, MOLAP, and ROLAP

An OLAP database (online analytical processing database) is used to perform data analysis. The data can come from any database but usually from a data warehouse because the data is configured for efficient access. An OLAP database is based on dimensions. We discuss dimensions later in this chapter but a quick example would be that a product can have a quantity, a price, a time of sale, and a place sold. These four items are the dimensions of the item product in this example. Where the dimensions of an object intersect is a single data item, for example, the sales of all cars in Denver for the month of July 2004 at a price greater than $100,000.00. One problem with OLAP databases is that the cubes formed by the relations between items and their dimensions can be sparse; that is, not all intersections contain data. This can lead to performance problems.

There are two versions of OLAP at last count: (1) MOLAP (multidimensional OLAP) and (2) ROLLUP (relational OLAP). The problem with MOLAP is that there is a physical limit on the size of the data cube, which can be easily specified. ROLAP allows the structure to be extended almost to infinity (the computer and OS limit sizes in modern database management systems). In addition to the space issues, a MOLAP uses mathematical processes to load the data cube, which can be time intensive. The time to load a MOLAP varies with the amount of data and number of dimensions. In the situation where a dataset can be broken into small pieces, a MOLAP database can perform quite well; but the larger and more complex the dataset, the poorer the performance. MOLAPs are generally restricted to just a few types of aggregation.

In ROLAP, the same performance limits that apply to a large OLTP come into play. ROLAP is a good choice for large datasets with complex relations. Data loads in a ROLAP can be done in parallel so they can be done quickly in comparison to a MOLAP that performs the same function.

Some applications use a combination of ROLAP and MOLAP to produce their results.

Using an Operational Database as a Data Warehouse

A common question is: Why do I need a separate database to perform data mining and reporting? Many current enterprise applications include data mining and knowledge tools that directly work on operational data. Some of these tools begin to blur the difference between an operational database and a data warehouse. For example, Oracle provides Report and Discoverer with many of its products. Both programs will not only use data in the local database, but will also access information in remote databases, including non-Oracle databases. These products combine some of the capabilities of data warehousing with the operational application. So, why create a separate data warehouse? The main reason is that one database cannot normally perform both functions. As discussed in Chapter 9, an online transaction processing application needs to execute transactions on a small amount of data quickly and efficiently, sometimes thousands of transactions per second. The knowledge tools and data mining work on very large sets of data, often taking hours or even days to complete a task. Although the database can easily be tuned to either OLTP or data warehouse, running both will affect the database system's performance. The reporting application would be moving large amounts of data through the database data cache, removing all the data used by the OLTP application. This would result in both applications having significant performance degradation.

Another reason that data warehouses are normally separate systems is because the data must be gathered from multiple, diverse systems. The data must be staged where it is transformed into usable information. Using the example above, the shipping database tracks items shipped. What happens when they pack five different products into one carton and ship it to the local office? There is no one-to-one relationship between products and shipping carton. The data is not usable in the current "operational" form.

Finally, because operational databases need to perform quickly, old data that is no longer needed by the application is routinely removed. Maintaining this data in the operational database will begin to affect its transaction performance. If the application needs a list of all orders that are still open or pending, the database can perform a full table scan. If there are closed orders from the past year still in the table, they will all be scanned. Removing closed orders from the past year will improve the performance of the database; however, this may be exactly the data the reporting system needs. That said, some companies do combine their operational systems with their data warehouses. If the database is of reasonable size, contains all the necessary data, and the server can handle the load, this can be a cost-effective system. By running as OLTP during office hours and running reports at night, the two operations can coexist. The DBA (database administrator) can also implement features to improve performance, such as archiving those closed orders from the past year in a separate or partitioned table. The remainder of this chapter focuses on database systems that implement a separate data warehouse.

GATHERING DATA

In designing a data warehouse, the data presents the classic chicken-and-egg scenario. Having large amounts of data will not necessarily allow one to determine relevant information. One needs to know what data one has and determine what information one can extract from it. Trying to define the type of information one wants without knowing what data one is starting with is impossible. During the design and building of the data warehouse, one may have to go back to some of the separate systems and make application (or database) modifications to maintain needed data. In the example used above, if the shipping department places orders in a carton based on the delivery location, without tracking which order went into which carton, one will not be able to track orders from inventory through shipping. Or worse, one might attempt to link cartons to orders by date and actually generate invalid reports that the company then uses to make decisions. In this case, one may need to look at how shipping can capture the order-to-carton relationship.

STAGING AND PROCESSING DATA

Staging data is an important and often overlooked step in operating the data warehouse. Because data comes from different systems, it must be transformed to fit into the data warehouse schema. In the early days of data warehousing, many companies simply loaded the data in the same form as it was maintained in the original system. The application then had to transform and link the separate groups of data during data mining. Although this method was inefficient from the standpoint of the database system, the real problem was improperly linking the data and producing erroneous results. For this reason, data is staged in a separate location — possibly a separate schema in the data warehouse database — transformed and validated, and then loaded into the actual data warehouse for analysis. In the earlier example, the shipping data was linked to actual order data in the inventory system and the local office system. Orders that did not have complete information would be moved out of the transformed data before being loaded into the warehouse. In this way, all the data in the warehouse is valid. Incomplete data is researched and, when valid, moved to be loaded. Invalid data may result from gathering data from different systems at different intervals. The inventory system may send data to the data warehouse every night, the local offices once a week, and the shipping department every two days. Thus, the data will arrive at the staging location at different times. As a complete set of data is validated as complete, it is loaded into the warehouse for analysis.

Staging and transforming the data can include aggregating information to support efficient reporting. If one reports the percent of orders filled by day, that report could require a significant amount of processing power every night to produce. If, instead, one aggregates that data in the staging location and loads the aggregates into the data warehouse along with the validated date, that report can become a simple query of the aggregate data (see Figure 10.1).

LOADING AND UNLOADING DATA

Once the data is validated, it must be loaded into the data warehouse from the staging area. This is normally accomplished using some type of bulk loading utility provided by the database system hosting the data warehouse. The procedure used to load data must be part of the warehouse design process and be flexible enough to operate efficiently as the data warehouse grows large.

Bulk load utilities provided by the database manufacturer will increase the loading speed; however, there are other actions the DBA can incorporate to improve loading speed. Normally, a data warehouse is stopped, the data is loaded, and then processing is resumed. Because the database is not processing reports, etc. during data loading, objects — such as indexes and materialized views — can be dropped to remove the database overhead of maintaining them. We have seen a case where a company estimated that at its current load rate, it would take 40 years to validate and load all the data. Removing all indexes and stopping the refresh of materialized views reduced the time estimate to less than six years, but there was obviously more work to do. Once loading is completed, the indexes are rebuilt, and the materialized views refreshed, the data warehouse can begin analyzing the data. There is a trade-off between the time spent loading the data and the time needed to rebuild indexes and materialized views.

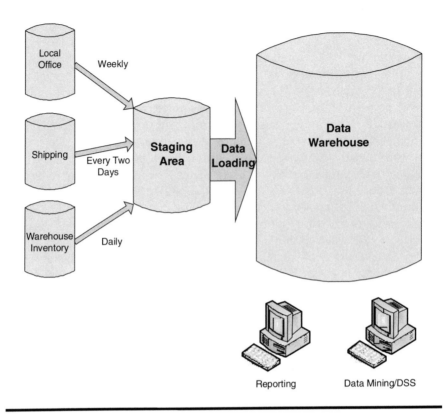

Figure 10.1   The data warehouse system.

Later in this chapter, we discuss partitioning the data within the data warehouse. If data is properly partitioned, one can load and unload data by pre-building the partition of new data and moving it into the database while removing the partition of no-longer-needed data. This is a very efficient method of moving data into and out of the data warehouse.

The data warehouse will eventually contain data that is no longer of value for the task it is performing. This data should be removed from the warehouse and archived. If one is using a partitioning method in the design, old data can be removed one partition at a time. Otherwise, one will be deleting unneeded data directly out of the database. Again, this process must be included as part of the system design. Unused data should be removed before new data is added. Again, indexes and materialized views can hinder delete performance; however, some indexes can improve delete performance. Before deleting a row, the database must find the row. Indexes that speed the location of the row to be deleted should be maintained during the delete process and then removed before loading new data. Again, as the data warehouse grows, the loading and unloading of data become more complex.

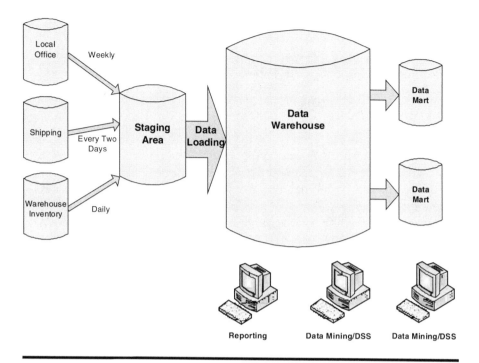

Figure 10.2   Data marts.

DATA MARTS

A data mart (see Figure 10.2) is a specialized form of a data warehouse that is designed to provide specific information. Normally, it is subject or application specific and differs from a data warehouse in the scope of the data it contains. A data mart can pull its data from a data warehouse or have data staged specifically for it. Data marts tend to be cheaper to design, build, and operate than a full data warehouse; however, they have a more limited analysis capability due to the focused nature of their data.

DESIGNING THE DATA WAREHOUSE

Chapter 9 discussed the design of online transaction processing systems that required fast execution involving small amounts of data. In a data warehouse, transactions normally involve vast amounts of data, requiring hours or possibly days to execute. Query performance is just as important when accessing large amounts of data, so the database must be designed and tuned specifically for the data warehouse. The first step in designing a data warehouse is determining what data is needed to meet the business requirements and if that data is available. Next, the schema must be designed that will provide efficient access to the data being analyzed. One note of caution: many times, a data warehouse is designed with a use in mind, but after the system is operational, additional capabilities are discovered and implemented. Flexibility is key.

Data Granularity

Data granularity is the level of detail at which data is stored in the data warehouse. This is a very important issue that must be addressed during design. Data should be maintained at the highest detail possible within system constraints. If the necessary level of data is not maintained, future requirements may necessitate that the schema be redesigned. For example, if product shipping times are aggregate to one number, pickup to delivery, then at a later time the company may need to know how much time was spent on processing, temporary storage, etc. That data will not be available and the company will have to redefine its requirements or redesign the data warehouse schema and wait until enough data has been gathered to conduct the analysis. On the other hand, if each step of the process is included in the data warehouse schema, a materialized view can be created that contains the aggregate shipping time to speed the current report.

Maintaining granular data allows different organizations to utilize the information in different ways. The information needed by the shipping department may be quite different from the reports required by the supply department, although both are utilizing the same data.

The issue of space, or volume of data, is always a problem in designing a data warehouse. If the volume of data becomes unmanageable, then one will be forced to aggregate in the staging phase and will lose the flexibility of granular data. The benefit of maintaining a high level of detail within the data dictionary is that the data warehouse can adapt to changes in the organization or application. One can always aggregate and pre-join data using materialized views to improve performance; but if the data is aggregated before loading it into the data warehouse, one will never be able to undo that aggregation. However, one must realize that having granular data that is then aggregated in the database may result in much of the data being stored twice in the database, thus increasing the space requirement.

Partitioning Data

Another major design issue is how to partition data. Partitioning data takes one large table and breaks it into smaller, easier-to-manage tables. This provides both an improvement in manageability and an improvement in query execution. In the example earlier in this chapter, our data warehouse contains orders. If our company executes thousands of orders a day in offices all over the country, the orders table will soon grow to an unmanageable level. By taking this large table and partitioning it into smaller tables, we can act directly on the partition with the data needed, instead of the one huge table.

There are even more benefits to partitioning than breaking large tables into smaller ones. Indexes are now smaller and materialized views can be based on a partition, if partitioned correctly, resulting in faster refreshes. This results in less I/O required to answer a query and less turbulence in the database data cache. Another benefit, as discussed earlier, is that data can be staged into partitions and efficiently moved into and out of the database.

Which Attribute to Partition On

There are two areas that need to be decided in the design phase relating to partitioning: what attribute to partition on and where to execute the partitioning. Because of the time-based nature of the orders, we might decide to partition the orders table by date.

```
OrdersJan2004
OrdersFeb2004
OrdersMar2004
```

By partitioning by date, we now look only in the OrdersFeb2004 table for those orders. We could also partition by order number: 1-99999, 100000 to 199999, 200000 to 299999, etc. Another method of partitioning would be by region or office branch: Orlando, Atlanta, Denver, Los Angeles, Seattle, Boston, etc. We can also partition the partitions. For example, we could use:

```
OrdersDenverJan2004
OrdersSeattleJan2004
OrdersDenverFeb2004
OrdersSeattleFeb2004
```

Again, the goal is to breakdown very large sets of data into smaller, more manageable sets while still maintaining the ability to access the entire large set. If one now needs to calculate total sales by office by month, one can total the sales data from each partition. If one needs a trend of total sales by month, one can still calculate the information across all the partitions.

The best way to partition the data is determined by analyzing how the data is accessed in the data warehouse. Most data warehouses track data first by date. This is because of the time-based nature of data analysis; however, this is not always the case. A telephone company would more likely partition on subscriber ID and then sub-partition by time. As one can see from the examples above, correctly partitioning the data can significantly improve data access, if it is by partition. Those queries that cross multiple partitions become less efficient.

Where to Partition

The second design decision concerning partitioning data is where to execute the partitioning. Here, there are two choices: (1) the application or (2) the database management system. Traditionally, it was recommended that partitioning be performed by the application. The application is aware that the orders are partitioned into separate tables and will access each table as needed to retrieve the needed data. There are a number of advantages in using application-level partitioning. First, the data definition does not need to remain the same in each partition. Because data maintained in a data warehouse can span many years, the definition of an order may change over time. The application can be written to extract the data from each partition based on its definition. The problem with application-level partitioning is that each application must know and understand differences in the data definition for each partition. The application also must query each partition separately to gather data across partitions. Because of recent capabilities being built into database management systems, these advantages are disappearing and the trend is moving toward allowing the database to manage partitions.

Database management system providers have watched the growth of data that their systems are being asked to manage. As a result, modern enterprise-level databases have powerful new capabilities to manage partitioned data. For example, if you create one partitioned table with five partitions for the years 2001, 2002, 2003, 2004, 2005, the definition would look something like this:

```
CREATE TABLE "SCOTT"."ORDERS" (
  "ORDER_NUM" VARCHAR2(10) NOT NULL,
  "ORDER_DATE" DATE NOT NULL,
  "ORDER_INFO1" VARCHAR2(10) NOT NULL,
  "ORDER_INFO2" VARCHAR2(10) NOT NULL,
  "ORDER_SALES" NUMBER(10, 2) NOT NULL,
  CONSTRAINT "PRI_KEY" PRIMARY KEY("ORDER_NUM"))
  TABLESPACE "USERS"
```

```
PARTITION BY RANGE ("ORDER_DATE") (
PARTITION "ORDERS_2001"
  VALUES LESS THAN  (TO_DATE('2001-12-31','YYYY-MM-DD')),
PARTITION "ORDERS_2002"
  VALUES LESS THAN  (TO_DATE('2002-12-31','YYYY-MM-DD')),
PARTITION "ORDERS_2003"
  VALUES LESS THAN  (TO_DATE('2003-12-31','YYYY-MM-DD')),
PARTITION "ORDERS_2004"
  VALUES LESS THAN  (TO_DATE('2004-12-31','YYYY-MM-DD')),
PARTITION "ORDERS_2005"
  VALUES LESS THAN  (TO_DATE('2005-12-31','YYYY-MM-DD'))
);
CREATE INDEX
  SCOTT.IDX_ORDERS
ON SCOTT.ORDERS ("ORDER_DATE")
LOCAL
;
```

The above command creates one logical table — the ORDERS table — in a database that consists of five physical tables. When one loads data, one simply inserts the data into the ORDERS table and the database management system will examine the ORDER_DATE and place the order in the correct partition. One drawback to using the database management system to maintain data partitions is that the definition of the data must remain the same across partitions. When faced with a change in the definition of an order, the data warehouse designer must determine if the new definition can be transformed during staging into the current definition or if a new, partitioned table must be created for the new data. In the worst case, the application should be modified to look in the two tables for order information, making the system a hybrid application/DBMS partitioned system. However, there are significant benefits to allowing the database to manage partition; indexing is one example. In the DDL above, a local index was created on the ORDERS table. The LOCAL clause tells the database to create a separate index for each partition. Having separate indexes for each partition will not help the query looking for an individual ORDER_NUM. For that one needs a GLOBAL index:

```
CREATE INDEX "SCOTT"."NUM_IDX"
    ON "SCOTT"."ORDERS"  ("ORDER_NUM");
```

The NUM_IDX index will be one large index that will span all partitions. When the query is looking for ORDER_NUM, it will use the GLOBAL index to find the rows it needs, then retrieve the rows from the table partitions. However, in the data warehouse, the one large index begins to have performance issues itself as it continues to grow. If this becomes a problem, one can partition the GLOBAL index using a different attribute than the table is partitioned by.

```
CREATE INDEX "SCOTT"."NUM_IDX"
    ON "SCOTT"."ORDERS"  ("ORDER_NUM") GLOBAL
    PARTITION BY RANGE ("ORDER_NUM") (
    PARTITION "NUM_LOW"
      VALUES LESS THAN  (10000) ,
    PARTITION "NUM_MID"
      VALUES LESS THAN  (20000) ,
    PARTITION "NUM_HIGH"
      VALUES LESS THAN  (30000) ,
    PARTITION "NUM_MAX"
      VALUES LESS THAN  (MAXVALUE) )
);
```

This example creates a logical index on the ORDER_NUM attribute that is composed of four physical indexes partitioned by the defined range. When a query is looking for a specific order number, such as 25467, it will access the NUM_IDX index, looking in the NUM_MID partition to locate the order. The database will then access the correct table partition to retrieve the data associated with order 25467. This is the advantage of having the database manage the partitions.

One partitioning method that the database will perform, one that would be difficult to implement within the application, is to create and maintain partitions based on a hash of an attribute. HASH partitions are commonly used to sub-partition a partition that has grown too large. For example, a telephone company could partition data based on telephone numbers. However, because every time someone picks up the phone, a record is created, a partition of 10,000 phone numbers might have millions of records. This partition can be sub-partitioned by a hash value on the phone number. This would create one logical table, containing multiple logical partitions, made up of many physical tables as sub-partitions. As one can imagine, the work associated with maintaining control and access to partitioning at this level in the application would be prohibitive. For that reason, most data warehouses are beginning to use either only database-managed partitioning or a combination of application-level partitioning and database partitioning. The example below shows part of the DDL needed to create the ORDERS table with partitions on ORDER_NUM, each partition containing 16 sub-partitions using the hash on ORDER_NUM:

```
CREATE INDEX "SCOTT"."NUM_IDX"
    ON "SCOTT"."ORDERS"   ("ORDER_NUM") GLOBAL
    PARTITION BY RANGE ("ORDER_NUM")
    SUBPARTITION BY HASH(ORDER_NUM)
      SUBPARTITIONS 16 (
    PARTITION "NUM_LOW"
      VALUES LESS THAN   (10000) ,
    PARTITION "NUM_MID"
      VALUES LESS THAN   (20000) ,
    PARTITION "NUM_HIGH"
      VALUES LESS THAN   (30000) ,
    PARTITION "NUM_MAX"
      VALUES LESS THAN   (MAXVALUE) )
);
```

The most powerful advantage to having the database manage data partitions is that the database will do the work of finding the correct partition to access the data. When one creates a partitioned table, the database knows the basis of the partitions. The application need not know that the table is partitioned. The application will query the ORDERS table, and the database will change the query to access only the appropriate partitions.

```
SELECT SUM(ORDER_SALES) FROM ORDERS
WHERE ORDER_DATE = TO_DATE('2002','YYYY');
```

The database knows that all the rows with a 2002 date will be in the ORDERS_2002 partition and will only access that partition to retrieve the results. By allowing the database to manage partitioning the data, one is further uncoupling the application from the physical data. This improves maintenance of both the application and the database.

Use of Keys

Another design issue is the use of keys within the data. Because data is gathered from multiple systems, there is a good chance that the separate systems use different keys. Furthermore, the keys used may change over time or keys could be reused. For this reason, when designing the data warehouse, it is recommended that you create keys within the data warehouse and convert the data to use the warehouse keys during staging. This will ensure that changes in one system do not result in invalid data in the data warehouse.

Normalization

There are many opinions on how a data warehouse should be normalized. Some contend that the data warehouse should be normalized to the same degree as any other type of database. Others believe that the data should be normalized using the dimensional form. For the most part, how one normalizes the data must be based on how one plans to use the data warehouse. Greater normalization provides for greater flexibility, but also increases overhead involved with joins and I/O. If the data warehouse supports multiple data marts, the data warehouse is normally normalized while the data marts are generalized to support their specific functions. More likely, the data warehouse will also be used like a data mart and there will need to be some trade-off between data normalization for flexibility and denormalization for performance. Most guidelines generally agree that the data warehouse should contain atomic data that is denormalized to improve performance and manageability. Data staging should transform the data from the separate normalized form to the data model used in the data warehouse. Data should be aggregated to improve performance but the granularity of the data must be maintained to support changes caused by business requirements.

If the data warehouse must remain as flexible as possible, data denormalization becomes the process of modifying the data in 3NF (third normal form) and combining tables to reduce I/O and improve performance. This process will result in redundant data that will improve select queries while adversely impacting updates and inserts. Because the data is normally not changed after loading, the negative impact of the redundant data has no effect on the data warehouse operations. Tables containing data that is constantly queried during database operations are candidates for pre-joining. Sequences of data that are constantly accessed can be placed in arrays. By combining and pre-joining tables, one can maintain data granularity and functional flexibility while dramatically improving query performance. Data that is rarely accessed should remain in separate tables. If the data warehouse has a specific business function and flexibility is not required, a more defined method of data modeling can be used, such as the dimensional model.

Dimensional Modeling

Most transaction databases are normalized to 3NF using entity-relationship diagrams. This allows for the compartmentalization of data and the removal of redundant data. Because a transaction tends to work on a small portion of the data at any one time, this method of normalization also provides improved performance and maintainability. The data warehouse tends to work on very large amounts of data. Normalizing the data to 3NF will result in complicated queries with multiple joins that are confusing to develop and perform poorly; users will be unable to create queries without extensive knowledge of the schema.

The dimensional model addresses these issues by organizing the data in a form that is easier for the user to understand and more efficient to query. The dimensional model is based on a central table, commonly called the fact table, that contains the data that is dynamic. Surrounding the fact table are the dimensional tables that contain data that normally does not change. The fact table is the largest, fastest growing table; there can be multiple fact tables in a data warehouse. Continuing the example from earlier in this chapter, the fact table would contain the order information. Each order would be represented by a row in the table containing such information as the order date, number of each product, shipping date, current status, etc. Surrounding this table are the dimension tables, such as the product table, containing information about products like name, manufacturer, weight, and size. The product table only changes when a product is updated, added, or deleted, while the fact table contains the data of every order and grows continuously. Because the schema tends to consist of a large table with many small tables around it, it is referred to as a *star schema*. The dimension tables are linked to the fact table by the data warehouse keys. The fact table would contain a column containing a product key. This key is probably unique to the data warehouse and is established during staging.

The dimensional model will also simplify data access by reducing the complexity of the schema. The fact table contains all the data changing over time, so most queries will focus on this table, joining to the dimension tables only to gather additional data. The actual design of the fact table is based on supporting the data warehouse's business function goals. Having all the data related to an order in one row of the fact table does result in some redundant data, but it also reduces I/O and simplifies the execution of queries. This simplified representation of the data allows users to develop relatively simple queries to extract the required data and improves performance by reducing the requirement to join multiple tables to locate the required data.

Pre-Aggregation

It is important that the granularity of the data be maintained when using the dimensional model. Because the data will continue to grow over time, it is important that the design maintains enough granularity to adapt to changes while still providing sufficient query execution performance. Pre-aggregating commonly used data can provide significant performance improvement. There are two common methods of pre-aggregating data in the warehouse. The first method involves pre-computing the data in the staging area and loading the aggregated data with the data load. This technique allows the data to be computed offline while the data warehouse is possibly still in use. Once ready, the data warehouse is stopped and the new data is loaded. Once it is validated, the data warehouse is placed back online for use. This method reduces the time the database is offline for the data load and only allows for aggregation of data in the stage location. Data already in the data warehouse cannot be included in the new aggregation. The second technique involves maintaining the aggregated data in the data warehouse and regularly re-computing it after the data load. This method involves creating procedures to aggregate the data using tables or materialized views, loading the data, re-computing the aggregates, and finally — after validating the data — placing the data warehouse back online. This technique allows not only for more complete aggregation of the data, but also extends the data load time because all the aggregations must be re-computed after the data is loaded from the staging area to the data warehouse. Actual data warehouses normally use a combination of both methods. Aggregations of data related to a single row of data to be loaded are normally performed in the stage location, while aggregations of multi-row data are performed in the data warehouse after the data is loaded.

As with partitioning discussed earlier, modern database management systems provide a number of enhanced capabilities to support aggregating data in the data warehouse. A table can be created to hold aggregate or pre-join data from the main tables. This can be executed and maintained manually or by the database using a materialized view. A materialized view is a physical table created based on a defined query. Unlike a normal view, the materialized view is a physical table that contains the data. The data contained in the materialized view can be queried directly from the materialized view like any other table. However, the database provides two important additional benefits to using materialized views to aggregate and pre-join data: (1) query optimization and (2) partial refreshes. The database optimizer is aware of the data stored in a materialized view. If a query requests information that the optimizer knows is already computed in the materialized view, it will change the execution of the query to use the pre-computed data in the materialized view. The second enhancement allows the materialized view to refresh only the changed data, reducing the refresh time. If the fact table contains millions of rows, completely refreshing a materialized view can take a considerable amount of time. If only a few hundred rows are added to the fact table, the database can refresh only the materialized view data affected by the new rows, thus greatly reducing the refresh time. Like partitioning, allowing the database to manage the pre-aggregation/pre-joining of data can provide improved performance while reducing the data loading time and improving the manageability of the system.

Protect the Data

The final design criteria that one must plan for is the protection of the data. The data warehouse contains the business information "jewels" and must be protected from both unintentional release and damage. All modern database management systems provide robust security capabilities and their implementation must be balanced between protecting the data and ensuring that valid users have access to the data. Data access security must be designed into the data warehouse from the beginning and reviewed often.

A more difficult issue is protecting the data itself. Again, all modern database management systems have the capability to recover from instance and hardware failure. The problem is that a company data warehouse with ten years of data could run into the multiple terabytes. Executing a full backup becomes prohibitive because it could take many days to complete. Other options must be explored to protect the data. All non-changing data (i.e., old data past the time when it will be updated) should be placed in read-only tablespaces that only need to be backed up once. Products that provide the ability to create incremental backups of changed data can also reduce the time required for backup. A more common approach is to protect the data using redundancy. Clustered hardware and large drive arrays provide hardware redundancy so that, if a component fails, the system will continue to function until it can be replaced or repaired. Triple-mirrored hard drives have a mean time to failure measured in decades. Oracle Real Application Clusters allow a database to continue to function even if servers in the cluster fail. Whichever method one chooses, one must evaluate it against the value of the data and the loss resulting from the data warehouse being offline.

SUMMARY

This chapter discussed the design considerations for a database implementing a data warehouse. The method used to stage the data and the data model used have a significant impact on the data warehouse's flexibility and performance. The key points in the chapter include:

1. The data warehouse must maintain the granularity of the data, so it can adapt to business changes over time.
2. The data warehouse schema must implement some denormalization to improve understandability and query performance. The data

model used is based on the business needs that the data warehouse supports. Combining and pre-joining tables increase performance while maintaining the flexibility to adapt to changing requirements. The dimensional model creates a more general schema, focused on the current business requirements. Data marts always use the dimensional model.

3. Data partitioning allows large tables to be split among smaller, more easily managed tables. Partitioning can be implemented in the application or by the database management system. Most data warehouses use a combination of database management of the partitions and application management of partitions caused by changes in the data.

4. Data warehouses must implement a strategy to protect the stored data. This includes security and fault tolerance/recovery schemes.

The data warehouse is a challenging system to design and maintain. The warehouse is designed to meet the business needs of the client; the design must maintain the flexibility to adapt to changing business needs. Recent improvements in enterprise database management systems allow the database to relieve the administrator and application of much of the data maintenance.

INDEX

Note: Italicized page numbers refer to illustrations and tables.